The Philosophy of Simondon

Pour Régine, qui a vu Simondon (le film) venir jusqu'à elle à Pasadena, ce qui nous a surtout permis de mieux nous connaître ... en espérant avoir l'occasion de revenir, en famille, la visiter dans son si beau pays.

Affectueusement,

Pascal

19 décembre 2014

The Philosophy of Simondon

Between Technology and Individuation

Pascal Chabot

Translated by Aliza Krefetz with the
participation of Graeme Kirkpatrick

B L O O M S B U R Y
LONDON • NEW DELHI • NEW YORK • SYDNEY

Bloomsbury Academic

An imprint of Bloomsbury Publishing Plc

50 Bedford Square	175 Fifth Avenue
London	New York
WC1B 3DP	NY 10010
UK	USA

www.bloomsbury.com

Originally published in French as La philosophie de Simondon © Pascal Chabot, 2003

This English language translation © Graeme Kirkpatrick and Aliza Krefetz

British Library Cataloguing-in-Publication Data
A catalogue record for this book is available from the British Library.

ISBN: HB: 978-1-7809-3032-9
PB: 978-1-7809-3311-5
ePub: 978-1-7809-3098-5
ePDF: 978-1-7809-3097-8

Library of Congress Cataloging-in-Publication Data
A catalog record for this book is available from the Library of Congress.

Typeset by Fakenham Prepress Solutions, Fakenham, Norfolk NR21 8NN
Printed and bound in India

Contents

Foreword

Graeme Kirkpatrick

Gilbert Simondon's philosophy is of growing interest to scholars in the English-speaking world. Pascal Chabot's book presents a clear and accessible account of Simondon's thought. This book was one of the first to be published in France at the start of the recent revival of interest in Simondon's philosophy, and it is the first monograph to appear on Simondon in English.

Simondon's fundamental concern is with technology, and he offers us a unique approach to understanding what it is and how it relates to other aspects of the human condition. His vision is profoundly subversive of commonsensical oppositions: he explores technology in relation to human invention and artifice while at the same time showing that its development has a profoundly natural, even holistic character. Drawing on cybernetics, depth psychology and historical studies, as well as philosophy, Simondon propounds a worldview that is both optimistic and critical. To grasp its potential we need a study like Chabot's, which puts his ideas into context and uses examples to show how they work.

Simondon presents an optimistic vision of technology development as a process that is, in its normal or natural unfolding, fundamentally integrative. This is what he calls 'concretization': designs combine elements to achieve a purpose, but in the process each element acquires new functions, and the overall design takes on a range that exceeds its designer's original intention. Chabot illustrates this process with numerous examples and draws the relevant contrasts with other modes of thought, such as Marxism and social evolutionism. His account is particularly clear when it comes to showing how, through concretization, the technological individual acquires a new unity all its own, and as such is neither mere artifice nor 'natural' in the standard sense of those terms.

Simondon also anticipates the relational turn which has dominated recent sociological thought. He argues that the individual cannot be understood independently of the 'pre-individual' and that we cannot conceptualize individuals, be they humans, crystals or refrigerators, as anything other than congeries of ongoing relationships. In their pre-individuated state the impress of informational codes determines what used to be thought of as the 'form' corresponding to a species or class of beings. As humans, we are shaped in this way by a variety of codes, and in this we do not differ from rock formations or other animals.

Unlike many contemporary theorists, however, Simondon does not infer from the ubiquity of informational codes that the human is merely an instantiation of code like any other 'technical individual'. Technical objects are always at bottom born of abstract reasoning, and as such they are not the same as natural creatures. The distinction we observe here is not the one that seems to be invoked most of the time when we distinguish technical from natural entities, things from humans. The two are intertwined in their genesis and in their being, and understanding this enables us to clarify what our 'humanist prejudices' actually are before we start to shed them. Chabot's text is exemplary here in setting out the issues as Simondon understood them and in positioning his argument against the relevant background in terms of both the technical changes associated with cybernetics and other philosophies that invoke a relational ontology.

The ideas of concretization and individuation result in a uniquely technological conception of humanity and of human problems. Simondon is a philosopher of technology but it is clear that his motivation for this orientation is based on the conviction that philosophy is, or ought to be, all about technology. There is nothing more 'natural' to humans than technical activity. Simondon combines a positive appreciation of technology as something valuable in itself with an understanding of nature that in many ways anticipates the green movement. For him, the inventor does not act against the world, but is better understood as working with elements of it to establish new kinds of coherence. The inventor-technologist is, like the artist, a seeker at the margins of society who tries to establish a different relationship to the world, alternative points of connection that can ultimately create new worlds for us to experience. For Simondon, technology has an integral aesthetic dimension, and technical action can be beautiful.

Translators' acknowledgements

Graeme Kirkpatrick thanks Sarah Carling and Pascal Chabot for their encouragement throughout the translation process. Thanks also to Arne De Boever for helpful comments on a draft of Chapter 3, and to Caroline Wintersgill for her support and encouragement.

Aliza Krefetz thanks François Lagarde and Pascal Chabot for introducing her to Simondon. She also thanks Leah Hewitt for her encouragement, as well as Sharon Krefetz, Elliott Krefetz and Suckbir Pal Singh Sangha for their support.

Introduction

Philosopher, amateur technologist, and Professor of Psychology at the Sorbonne, Gilbert Simondon produced a wide-ranging and original body of work. In a time of increased specialization and compartmentalisation of knowledge within disciplines, he worked towards a global vision of the connections between technology, science, psychology and philosophy. In the tradition of the encyclopaedists of the French Enlightenment, Simondon strove to produce a concrete philosophy that could confront problems of technology and society, cultural movements, and the evolution of psychology. He developed a philosophy of the emotions and sought to understand the consequences of technological change for civilizations. Inspired as much by Ionian physiology as by cybernetics, his was a philosophy of singularities. The encyclopaedists sought to trace the circumference of the sphere that encompasses all human knowledge. For Simondon, the centre of this ever-widening sphere is philosophical wonder. Wonder at the origins of natural and technological phenomena, channelled into a systematic interrogation of the processes that engender and perpetuate them.

Simondon was born on 2 October 1924 at Saint-Etienne in France, and died in 1989. Admitted to the École Normale Supérieure in 1944, he went on to teach philosophy at the Lycée Descartes in the city of Tours, from 1948 to 1955. During his tenure at the school he substituted for the physics instructor whenever possible, and inducted his students into the workings of the numerous machines and electronic devices which he had installed in the school's basements. In 1960, he became a professor at the University of Poitiers, where he established a psychology laboratory. In 1963, he was appointed to the Sorbonne, where he again led the psychology lab. Not all of his time, however, was devoted to libraries and laboratories. He was also the father of seven children. His entire oeuvre bears witness to an extreme sensitivity to nature and a level of erudition befitting a true Renaissance man.[1]

Simondon saw himself first and foremost as a teacher and researcher, and invested little effort into overseeing the publication of his work. The somewhat roundabout manner in which his doctoral thesis was published bears testament to this. His first book, which was to remain his best-known work, was published in 1958. *Du mode d'existence des objets techniques* (*On the Mode of Existence of Technical Objects*) was only a supplementary appendix to his doctoral thesis. His second book, *L'individu et sa genèse physico-biologique* (*The Physico-Biological Genesis of the Individual*), which constituted the first part of his primary thesis, was published in 1964 and reissued in 1995. The second part of this thesis, *L'individuation psychique et collective* (*Psychic and Collective Individuation*), did not appear until 1989, twenty-five years later.

The gaps between these dates make it clear that Simondon's work was, for decades, in a kind of 'purgatory'.[2] It was rarely cited during his lifetime, except by the sociologist Georges Friedmann and, most famously, by the philosopher Gilles Deleuze. The philosophy of technology interested few in France at the time. It was a Canadian senator and specialist in mechanical engineering, Jean Le Moyne, who was the first to ask for a public interview with Simondon. The

---

[1] As attested to by M. Mouillaud in the *Annuaire 1990 des Anciens Élèves de l'École Normale Supérieure* (*1990 Alumni Directory of the École Normale Supérieure*), p. 3.

[2] G. Hottois, *Simondon et la philosophie de la 'culture technique'*, Brussels: De Boeck, 1993.

response to Simondon's philosophical reflections was fairly subdued. He gave only two interviews in total. The second, published in the literary magazine *Esprit* in 1983, was an appeal to 'save the technical object'.

Simondon retired from teaching in 1984, and it was not until six years later, one year after his death, that *Cahiers Philosophiques* devoted a special issue to his work. In 1991, the phenomenologist Jacques Garelli dedicated considerable space to Simondon in his book *Rhythms and Worlds*. In 1992, an English translation of some twenty pages from the introduction to his thesis on the individual appeared in a New York publication, *Incorporation*, which brought together studies of cinema, cyberculture and philosophy. The following year, Gilbert Hottois published the first book devoted solely to Simondon's work. In 1994, another special issue, this time in the journal of the *Collège International de Philosophie*, signalled Simondon's rise to philosophical notoriety. More articles on Simondon's work began to appear. In 1999, Muriel Combes published her book *Simondon. Individu et collectivité (Simondon: Individual and Collective)*, subtitled *Pour une philosophie du transindividuel (For a trans-individual philosophy)*. In 2002, some of my colleagues and I put together a volume of studies on Simondon for Éditions Vrin, and Jacques Roux published papers from a colloquium at Saint Etienne under the title *Gilbert Simondon: Une Pensée Opérative (Gilbert Simondon: Operational Thought)*.

Why this interest after three decades of silence? What has made Simondon suddenly relevant? He brought something new to philosophy: a way of thinking about the modes of existence of individuals and objects. To speak of the 'mode of existence' of an *individual* supposes that there are also modes of existence that are not individuated. The world is more than a sum of individuals. We live in a network where the pre-individual plays a significant role. Simondon speaks also of a mode of existence of technical objects. He means by this that the object is more than just *any thing*. The product of an invention, it is defined by its relationship with an environment that it also modifies.

This is the singularity of Simondon's philosophy. Possessing a rare capacity for detached contemplation, he moved beyond established controversies to explore truly novel territory. The period during which he wrote saw the rise of two groups with opposing attitudes towards the role of technology in modern society: the technocrats and the first ecologists. He addressed his most severe criticisms to the technocrats, whose view of technology as a commodity to be exploited for power and profit filled him with horror. His attitude towards the nascent ecology movement was more nuanced. There is, running through his philosophy, an idea of the spontaneous creativity of nature, inspired by the teachings of the Pre-Socratics. Having devoted extensive study to all manner of natural phenomena, he firmly supported the ecologists' respect for natural cycles and their devotion to the preservation of endangered species, but he rejected their antagonism towards science and technology.

Simondon's position in this debate is undeniably original. He is philosophically incapable of siding with one particular camp. The objective of his philosophy, in essence, is to establish connections between what appear to be opposing forces. His writings often evoke a sense of *coincidentia oppositorum*. He sees invention as the productive manifestation of a union of opposites. Relationships also occupy a central place in his philosophy of nature and humanity, which he described as a 'philosophy of individuation'. For Simondon, the complexity of the relations involved in this process of individuation is a source of wonder.

The centrality of relations is something that Simondon intuits, and the concept of intuition is itself a central aspect of Simondon's philosophical approach. It is at once general, of cosmic dimensions, and local, on the level of the individual. It is neither deduced from sound principles nor constructed based on single operations. This singular intuition is unique to Simondon, although close in certain respects to Bergson and in others to Rousseau. It brings a stunning richness to his vision of the world, a sensitivity to transformations and interactions between the individual and non-individuated modes of being. The ideal that inspires Simondon's philosophy is one of harmony or, more precisely, resonance between nature, humans and human technology.

In the first part of this book, we will examine some important moments in the history of technology, as illuminated by Simondon's philosophy: The encyclopaedia of Diderot and d'Alembert, Marx and the industrial revolution, and cybernetics. We will engage with questions of progress and alienation, economy and memory.

The second part is devoted to the concept of individuation. Bricks, crystals, coral colonies, the psyche, the collective and the imagination are examples taken by Simondon to demonstrate the impact of becoming and of time on individuals.

Finally, the third part attempts to bridge the gap between individuation and technology. It poses fundamental questions: What was the influence of Jungian psychology on Simondon's thought? How should we interpret his vision of a convergence between technology and the sacred? And if there is such a thing as technological 'progress', should we conceive of a parallel moral 'progress'?

Part One

Philosophy of Technology

1

The Object

Genesis of the technical object: The process of concretization

The wheel

The first traces of the wheel are Mesopotamian. A Sumerian pictogram, dated to 3500 BC, shows a cart with wheels. It is unknown whether the wheel was invented in a single place, then taken to others (once seen in action, it would be hard to forget), or whether it was invented in different places by independent civilizations. The latter hypothesis is also probable, despite the fact that the Pre-Columbians never developed the concept, nor did they use animals to transport heavy loads.

The wheel is a true invention. Unlike other technologies, it does not imitate an animal property. Whereas pincer utensils echo structures found in molluscs, and flying devices are isomorphic with the bodies of birds, the structure of the wheel, ingeniously designed to facilitate the transfer of forces, is not present in any animal. Bionics specialist R. Boucart offers an explanation. He points out that the organization of animals' bodies requires permanent connections for the circulation of blood and transmission of nerve impulses. The shape of the wheel precludes the possibility of any permanent connection with its axis. In a living being equipped with wheels, blood vessels and nerves 'would be rapidly destroyed by constant torsion'.[1]

Nevertheless, nature is full of circular movements (snowballs, the movement of celestial bodies, rockslides, rolling twigs, etc.) which could have served as a model for systems that employ a rolling or turning motion, such as the potter's wheel. The uncertainty that surrounds the birth of the wheel testifies to a characteristic feature of invention: it is the product of manipulation, perception, imagination, imitation, intuition and luck. This is why research into the art of invention is a much larger quest than it at first appears. To seek a formula for invention is to seek a formula for all of humanity and its history.

Simondon's *Course on the Invention and Development of Technologies* (*Cours sur l'invention et le développement des techniques*)[2] contains an analysis of the genesis of the wheel. Simondon's writing style was informed by his youthful reading of the popular science magazine *Science et Vie* (*Science and Life*). His analysis of the wheel preserves a felicitous – and old-fashioned – union of language and technical description:

> As a mediator between a heavy load and the path along which it is to travel, the vehicular wheel first appears in the form of a series of rollers or logs. As a mediator, this system is, in principle, perfect. With no central axle, there is no friction, but there is also no system of autocorrelation between the rollers and the load being carried: the load moves forward at twice the speed of the rollers. An operator is needed, therefore, to recycle the rollers, replacing them one by one in front of the load, to keep it moving forward. The wheel with axle and

---

[1] R. Boucart, 'Bionique', in *Encyclopédie Universalis*.

[2] Translator's note: in French, the words 'technologie' and 'technique' are used more or less interchangeably to refer to technology, with the latter term being somewhat more general and more often applied to technologies that pre-date industrialization. In this translation, we have generally chosen to translate 'technique' as 'technology' (or 'technological' when used as an adjective), unless the context clearly indicates that a broader meaning is intended.

hub is, in contrast, perfectly correlated with the movement of the load, through the mediation of the vehicle that it transports: it is like a roller that is always in position. However, it loses some of the efficacy of a true roller, because the axle and hub system produces friction (which in turn produces heat, resulting in wear and tear, and necessitating the application of water or animal fat – the first lubricants[3]). The synthesis of these two stages of development was eventually achieved in the development of wheels with ball-bearings, which transpose the system of rollers to the hub of the wheel. Arranged in a circular formation within the hub, the rollers recycle themselves without an operator. Autocorrelation, added at the second stage of vehicular development, interfered with the perfect mediation characteristic of the first stage. But in the wheel with ball-bearings, the autocorrelation between wheel and external structure is maintained while the perfect mediation of the rollers is incorporated into the internal structure of the wheel. Technological progress is achieved through a dialectical relationship between mediation (adaptation to the end terms: the path to be travelled and the load to be carried) and autocorrelation, the relation between the technical object and itself.[4]

The concept of autocorrelation, as it applies to the genesis of the wheel, complicates the analysis of mediation. Correlation designates the inter-dependence of two elements (here the load to be carried and the path to be travelled). The idea of mediation already implies a correlation between two terms. The prefix 'auto-' adds another idea. It indicates that the correlation is realized by the wheel itself. This may, at first, seem a trivial notion. However, the concept of autocorrelation allows us to understand that the wheel fulfils multiple functions simultaneously. In the first phase of development of the wheel, autocorrelation between the

[3] Simondon uses the French term *axonge*, which refers to rendered animal fat, as from the stomach of a sheep (*suif* in French) or from a pig (*saindoux*, or lard, in English). The author provides the etymology of the word *axonge*, which comes from the Latin *axungia*, a compound of the words *axis* (axle) and *ungere* (to anoint; to cover with oil). In Latin, *axungia ponere* means 'to lubricate'.

[4] G. Simondon, *L'invention et le développement des techniques (Invention and development of technologies)*, course taught from 1968 to 1970, p.13 (published in 2005, *Cours et conférences*, Éditions le Seuil).

load to be carried and the path to be travelled is imperfect because an external operator must move the rollers from back to front. There is a correlation between the terms, but it does not extend to the function of switching the rollers. When the wheel becomes a system with an axle and hub, it takes on both functions: the correlation of terms and the switching of the rollers. The external operations (switching the rollers, and later, greasing the axle) are integrated into the structure of the wheel.

Autocorrelation is, thus, a function fulfilled by a structure while acting upon the same structure, allowing it to fulfil this same function a second time. The wheel turns itself. This description demonstrates how a technical mechanism, once established, can maintain its own momentum. The wheel is a mediation which, through a system of internal bearings, perpetuates its own mode of existence.

The locomotive

'The individual technical object is not such and such a thing given here and now (*hic et nunc*), but something that has a genesis'.[5] The genesis of an object is a process of refinement (*perfectionnement*). This notion is often defined in terms of usefulness or profitability. But Simondon rejects such external criteria of success, which obscure the essential nature of the technical object. That an object is more profitable or effective is only a secondary consequence of its refinement. This is why he invokes a process internal to the development of technical objects: the refinement of the object is a 'concretization'.

Invention begins with a primitive, abstract form. Simondon explains this as follows:

> There exists a primitive form of the technical object, its *abstract form*, in which each theoretical and material unit is treated as an absolute,

⁵ G. Simondon, *Du mode d'existence des objets techniques*, Paris: Aubier, 1958, p. 20; reissued in 1969, 1989 and 2001. The version cited is the 1989 edition.

with its own intrinsic perfection, which must be constituted as a closed system in order to function.[6]

In the abstract form of the locomotive, each sub-system is independent, as the vehicle's history demonstrates. As early as the sixteenth century, rails were laid inside mines to facilitate the transport of coal. At the bottom of the mine and at the pit-head, coal wagons, pulled by animals or by men, circulated on wooden tracks. In the eighteenth century, iron rails replaced the wooden tracks, which wore out quickly due to friction. At the centre of a coal-mine is a narrow shaft that connects the galleries to the open air. Through this shaft, the miners ascend and descend, the coal is lifted, the mine is ventilated, and water is pumped from the galleries. These activities all coexist within a single narrow passageway. To prevent them from interfering with one another, they must be streamlined as much as possible. The mine is a hotbed of invention because it is a hotbed of problems. The flux of workers, animals, gas and coal must be appropriately channelled. It was in this context that the steam-engine was developed. Stationed above ground, it powered the water pumps and ventilation systems, which had previously been operated by water wheel.

Eventually, the idea arose to combine these elements. The steam-engine was mounted on a wagon. A crankshaft transmission system converted the alternation of the engine's pistons into a continuous turning of the wagon's wheels.[7] Primitive locomotives combined different existing technologies, but this combination was as yet 'intellectual', closer to the freedom of theory than to material practicalities. None of the components were originally conceived to function together. The structure of each element betrays its original intended purpose. The steam-engine adapted to power the wagon was originally designed to be fixed in place. In this position, its weight

---

[6] *Idem*, p. 21.
[7] *Cf.* on this subject G. Basalla, *The Evolution of Technology*, Cambridge: Cambridge University Press, 1990, p. 90.

was unimportant. A steam-engine contains a water-filled boiler, heated from below by a fire-box. In stationary versions, this boiler was surrounded by a wall of fire-bricks which retained heat, since the position of the fire-box made it vulnerable to heat loss. When the machine was fixed in place at the entrance to the mine, its size and weight were of little consequence, as long as it effectively performed its intended function. However, for the construction of the locomotive, the problem of weight and size had to be addressed: it was impossible to build a retaining wall on a wagon.

Technological invention consists of assembling a coherent system from disparate elements. The transformation conceived of by Marc Seguin attests to this. Seguin invented the fire-tube boiler. Submerged in this boiler's water tank were tubes which collected the hot gas released from the fire-box. By placing the heat source inside the boiler, Seguin reversed the older design, increasing the surface area for heat transfer while reducing the amount of water required to generate steam. A fire-brick frame was no longer needed to prevent heat loss. The weight of the engine was reduced. But Seguin's invention had additional benefits. The tubular boiler also allowed for a reduction in the size of the fire-box, since the heat it produced was conserved inside the tubes. This type of boiler would be used in the first series of locomotives constructed by George and Robert Stephenson, beginning in 1823. The earliest model in this series made its first journey in 1825 on the newly constructed Stockton–Darlington line, travelling at an average speed of 12.4 miles per hour while hauling a 90-tonne load.[8]

---

[8] In a study of the evolution of railway wagons in the nineteenth century, Lorenz writes: 'One could almost believe oneself to be studying the results of a process of phylogenetic differentiation. (…) These examples clearly demonstrate the absence of prior planning in the evolution of what we might call the products of civilization. They are developed in response to specific needs, just like biological organs, and the parallel between their historical development and the phylogenetic differentiation of biological structures strongly lends itself to the idea that analogous factors come into play in both processes and that, above all, selection, and not rational planning, plays the primary role', (cited

Seguin's invention is an example of concretization. It allowed for multi-functionality. Rather than serving a single function, each element of the invention acquires a plurality of functions: the tubes heat the water and are channels of combustion and heat exchange. The external wall of the boiler also assumes the function of the original brick frame. The effects of the invention exceed the formulation of the initial problem:

> Concretization brings not only new properties, but complementary functions, beyond those sought after, which we might call 'superabundant functions'. (...) These properties of the object surpass expectations; it is a partial truth to say that an invention's *purpose* is to attain an objective, to produce an entirely predictable effect. An invention is brought into being in response to a problem, but its effects extend beyond the resolution of the problem, due to the superabundant efficacy of the created object when it is a true invention.[9]

Concretization may be understood as the unification of certain fundamental concepts: synergy, superabundant functionality, coherence, internal resonance and formalization.

Mode of existence of the concrete object

Once in operation, the technical object frees itself from its inventor. Its superabundant functionality separates it from any plans or intentions projected on to it. The object acquires a concrete character, an internal coherence. For Simondon, it is necessary to acknowledge this as a mode of existence, a way of evolving, with its own rules

---

by T. Gaudin, in *De l'Innovation*, Paris: L'Aube, 1998, pp. 61–2). This argument resonates with Simondon's explanations of genesis. The processes are inherent to the invention of the object and only secondarily constrained or informed by planning.
[9] G. Simondon, *Imagination et invention*, course material (hand-out) published in the *Bulletin de Psychologie*, December 1965, pp. 395–414, February 1966, pp. 916–29, and March 1966, pp. 1074–95, p. 1197 (published in 2008, *Editions de la Transparence*).

and constraints. This mediation is one in which the object gains autonomy. It cannot be summed up in terms of either human intentions or natural processes.

It is one of Simondon's recurring themes that the philosophy of technology lags well behind technological developments. Its points of reference are still Descartes' simple machines, equipped with winches, hoists and pulleys; Archimedes' screw; and the Enlightenment Era tools catalogued in Diderot and d'Alembert's *Encyclopaedia*. Simondon seeks to revitalize philosophical thought by turning his attention to more recent technological advancements, the products of a history that has largely escaped philosophical scrutiny. He does the same with the concept of artifice. In philosophy, this concept has remained unchanged since antiquity. For the Greeks, artifice was 'that which is produced by man and not spontaneously engendered by nature'. Art, which the Greeks identified with ποίησις (*poiesis*) 'creation' and technology, from the Greek τέχνη (techne) 'craft' are the two great sources of artifice. The 'artificial' nature of technology accounts for its ostracism, its classification as an inferior activity, useful, but in no way a manifestation of that which is noblest in human expression. Art had to justify its 'poietic', creative character, as witnessed by the medieval disputes over whether attempts to imitate nature through artificial means constitute blasphemy. This debate persisted until the Baroque era, when the issue was at last resolved with the embrace of an exaggerated, highly ornamented style, such that resemblance between art and nature was no longer a point of concern. The twentieth century moved beyond this question with the development of forms of artistic expression that were no longer concerned with copying nature. The art of the twentieth century strove to capture the essence of nature, not its image. Its emphasis on expressive intensity and rawness of style brings it closer to the arts of other civilizations where artifice is imbued with a life force of its own, as in the case of fetish objects.

Technology, however, is still perceived as a source of artifice. Simondon wanted to move the discussion of technology beyond this idea. If the abstract technical object is artificial, the concrete technical object is not. This realization necessitates a paradigm shift: the classification of an object as natural or artificial no longer depends on its origin. The difference is no longer framed as a dichotomy between spontaneous, natural generation and laborious human production. What matters is whether the mode of existence of the object is abstract or concrete. The abstract technical object is artificial. The concrete technical object 'approximates the mode of existence of natural objects.'[10]

This conception of the difference between life and artifice may also be applied to things considered natural. The hothouse flower that produces only petals and never fruit is the product of an artificial plant. Man has made it artificial by depriving it of its biological rhythms and by rendering it dependent. This plant would not be able to survive on its own. It has lost its capacity to resist cold, drought, or exposure to the sun. It produces only flowers, never seeds. This 'artificialization' of nature aligns with Simondon's definition of artificiality: 'artificiality is that which is intrinsic to the artificializing action of man, whether this action affects a natural object or an object that is entirely man-made.'[11]

Simondon is careful not to take this point too far. He never asserts that the mode of existence of technologies is entirely commensurate with that of living things. Concretization is a tendency within the development of technical objects. The object always retains the vestiges of its abstract and artificial origins. Its existence presupposes an objective conceived of and executed by human beings. What

---

[10] *Mode d'existence*, p. 46.
[11] *Idem.*

Simondon does, quite simply, is to blur the boundary between that which is artificial and that which is alive.

The inventor

The inventor has a sense of the future and is therefore a historical being. Mircea Eliade, cited by Simondon, described the recent advent of historical self-awareness in modern societies, explaining why 'moderns' prefer invention to adaptation.

Invention was forbidden in archaic societies: it upset the cosmic order. Traditional peoples had cosmogonies that told of the birth of the world and the life of the gods. They imitated these mythical narratives. Their acts took on meaning, 'reality', only insofar as they repeated the acts long ago performed by the gods or the ancestors. The warrior is brave because the sacred warrior proved his bravery *in illo tempore*: in the mythical time of origins. Objects and actions derive their value from the fact that they participate in a reality that transcends them. Nutrition is not a simple, physiological operation: it renews a communion. Marriage and orgies alike echo mythical prototypes. 'They are repeated', writes Eliade, 'because they were consecrated in the beginning ... by gods, ancestors, or heroes'.[12] The world is the reflection of a higher order: according to Mesopotamian beliefs, the Tigris has its model in the star Anunit and the Euphrates imitates the star of the Swallow.[13] Human constructions respect this transcendent order. When David gives his son Solomon the plans for the temple buildings, the holy of holies and all their utensils, he assures him that 'all this ... the Lord made me understand in writing

---

[12] M. Eliade (trans. Willard R. Trask), *The Myth of Eternal Return*, New York: Pantheon Books, 1965, p.15.

[13] Translator's note: in Babylonian astronomy, Anunit (or Anunitum) corresponds to the modern constellation of Andromeda, while the Great Swallow consists of the southwest portion of Pisces, plus the star Epsilon Pegasi.

by his hand'.[14] David did not claim to be inventing something: he was following a celestial model.

This existence based on repetition and adaptation to archetypes is not historical. It does not bear the mark of time; it proceeds as if historical time were an illusion, a phenomenon of little interest. The passing days are not a burden. They are simply a backdrop against which is projected the return of a sacred, mythical past. The passing years do not induce melancholy, because the world is reborn with each repetition of the natural cycle. Archaic societies occupy an eternal present.

Historical consciousness is revolutionary. It abolishes this cycle of time. Nothing more returns and nothing is repeated: the future is to be invented. Eliade traces this turning point back to Abraham. Beginning with his journey into the desert, history opens like a path. Time becomes linear. Man becomes aware of an eschatology. He is freed from the unchanging certainties guaranteed by the eternal return of the same endlessly repeating cycles. He enters into a new dimension and realizes that he is capable of progress.

This revolution has a resounding impact upon technology. It, too, becomes historic. The smith no longer receives his skill from the gods and makes swords for warriors who assume the role of the mythic heroes. From now on he will work his iron freely, unconstrained by mythical archetypes.

Invention is 'the discovery of a system of compatibility that constitutes a higher level on which previously incompatible and disparate elements can be integrated'.[15] The inventor is a man of action.[16] He

---

[14] I Chronicles, 28.19.

[15] *L'invention et le développement des techniques* (*The invention and development of technologies*), *op. cit.*, p. 89.

[16] The inventor is presented here as a lone individual. He is closer to the fictional geniuses in certain Jules Verne stories than to contemporary researchers in techno-science. Simondon sometimes registers an interest in collective research, but his tendency is to single out the inventor as a 'pure individual' (*cf.* Part Three of this volume). For a critique of the figure of the lone genius inventor see T. Gaudin, *De l'innovation* (*On Innovation*), *op. cit.*

rejects adaptation: he judges it meagre and insufficient, since it does not create new dimensions. Rather than adapt to cold water, he invents a way to boil it. Adaptation does not change the means of becoming; it merely repeats and reproduces. Doctrines which insist that the essential activity of living things is adaptation assume that there exists, in the surrounding environment, some goal to be attained. Obstacles separate the subject from what he wants, obliging him to adapt as best he can to the forces that surround him. He either uses his cunning to circumvent these obstacles, or allows himself to be carried along.

Simondon's inventor has a different conception of existence. He is not a man of conflict. He opposes nothing. He integrates. He doesn't seek to attain a specific goal, he attempts to find order and connection across the different worlds that he inhabits. For the inventor, there is not only 'a food object or a prey object, but a world of nourishment and a world of avoiding predators, or a world of sexuality'.[17] These worlds overlap and encroach upon one another. They are not radically heterogeneous, but neither can they be neatly superimposed, one atop the other. Their coexistence is not a given, but rather a problem to be overcome. This problem, manifest in the tension that precedes choice, the *fluctuatio animi* of which Spinoza wrote, implies a choice and an *action*.

For Simondon, the individual invents – and invents technologies in particular – because, fundamentally, he must invent in order to establish coherence in the world. Without invention, without this action which is the very essence of becoming, the individual is 'faced with a world that doesn't coincide with him', because it is plural, disparate. For the inventor, 'the complete universe'[18] is yet

---

[17] G. Simondon, *L'individu et sa genèse physico-biologique* (*The physico-biological genesis of the individual*), Paris: P.U.F., 1964. The edition cited is from the reissue by J. Million, 1995, Grenoble, p. 210.

[18] *Idem*, p. 203.

to be constructed: the movement towards integration must begin again each day and be taken further. Problems are resolved without the need to directly oppose or contradict them. Their solution again emerges at a higher level, a network of solutions into which can be integrated disparate and isolated elements, whose potential functions cannot be known as long as they remain outside this network. The inventor works to establish communication, to recover a complete universe that is not lost in a mythic past, but is projected into a still unrealized future. Invention functions as a promise of pacification without war, in which 'each step ... presents itself as the solution to the previous states'.[19]

The 'coherence of the world' must be invented because, for a technical consciousness, such coherence is not ensured by any transcendent myth. What coherence, then, have technologies invented? Or, to phrase the question in more Simondonian terms, what processes or qualities of technology might govern the establishment of such coherence?

[19] *Idem.*

2

Technological Encyclopaedism

Technology grows up

A child's initiation into the world of technology begins as an instinctive and ritualized engagement with the technical object. Passed down from generation to generation, traditional technical knowledge is grounded in long-established practices and ancient customs. The gesture is essential. Turns of hand are kept secret: difficult to explain, they are shared only within select groups, who jealously guard their technical skills.

A technological childhood is a courageous one. It is a dangerous hand-to-hand struggle with the world. Technology must learn in its infancy to resist nature, to survive sandstorms and floods. Technologies are counter-entropic: they hold the chaos of the elements in check. They exist at the outer limit of human adaptability. When they succeed, they neutralize natural dangers, and above all, the danger posed by man himself when he is afraid. 'There is a body to be mastered', writes Jankélévitch, 'a frightened animal whose instinctual terror may at any moment contradict and override man's learned habituation to danger'.[1] Hence the need for the tests and initiation rites that mark entry into a technical trade.

---

[1] V. Jankélévitch, *Traité des vertus*, vol. II, *Les vertus et l'amour*, I, Paris: Flammarion, 1986, p. 95.

Technologies are sacred. The art of making tools is essentially superhuman, divinely or demonically inspired. Minerals must be extracted from the earth in which they grow, according to many traditional beliefs. Fire must be tamed, providing the means to speed up natural processes, and to fashion the products of nature into something unnatural. The successful fulfilment of these tasks gives *homo faber* a magical aura. He is often viewed as the heir to those mythical heroes who founded human civilization, since he collaborates in the work of creation. He is feared and respected. His tools are themselves invested with magical powers. In symbolic thought, the object is always more than itself. It is a sign or receptacle of something else, of a reality that transcends the material level.

For Simondon, the *Encyclopaedia*, product of the eighteenth century French Enlightenment, announced the end of the traditional system. It introduced a consciousness of progress into communities previously marked by their continuity, their stability, the permanence of their institutions and the repetition of their gestures. Multiple factors account for the lack of evolution prior to this point: the influence of natural rhythms on the rhythms of life and on the physical and intellectual routines of individuals;[2] the radical constraints of geography, which acts as a catalyst or a limiting factor; the need for human input at each stage of technical production, due to inefficient means of transmission; limited availability of fuel and raw materials; the stability of professional roles and traditional trades.[3] The creators of the *Encyclopaedia* set out to combat these forces. A new era was beginning: technology was growing up.

[2] *Cf.* G. Friedmann, *Sept études sur l'homme et la technique*, Paris: Denoël, 1966, pp. 18–19.

[3] *Cf.* J. Walch, *Introduction à la philosophie de la civilisation*, Paris: Vrin, 1980, p. 38. The second chapter of Walch's book discusses this connection. He demonstrates that the illusion of permanence masks an underlying tension between 'the individual initiative of the artisan and the conscious desire for progress among the educated and ruling classes'. There is a lack of diffusion of technological progress in traditional societies, which helps to account for the rigidity of their social structures.

Maturity

The *Encyclopaedia* of Diderot and D'Alembert (1751–72) was the "'Fête de la Fédération" of technologies'.[4] For the first time, the unity of technologies was made visible. The *Encyclopaedia* encompassed all that was known of reality. Its etymological origins, from the Greek κύκλος (*kuklos*), 'circle', reflected the ambitions of its creators: to assemble all the world's knowledge within its sphere. Technologies that had previously operated in isolation were now gathered together. Diderot fought against the compartmentalization perpetuated by trade guilds. Geographical distance, family traditions and rivalries kept technologies within a closed system. 'It is necessary,' insisted Diderot, 'to divulge all secrets without exception'.[5] Progress requires communication. The idea was that one invention could inspire others. It was the men of letters, not the artisans, who took the task of diffusion upon themselves. They formed a community of researchers who championed a new mentality.

The *Encyclopaedia* propagated inventions in a spirit of universality. In an article on *Les limites du progrès humain (the limits of human progress)*, Simondon put forward a hypothesis to explain the 'universalizing power' of technologies: their capacity to spread across culturally diverse regions is due to their 'primitiveness'. Over the course of history, three successive systems came to dominate the Western world: language, religion and technology. There was a marked evolution – or devolution – from language, crucial to the rise of the Greek city-state, to religion, the centre of medieval

---

[4] *Mode d'existence*, p. 94. Translator's note: The 'Fête de la Fédération' on 14 July 1790 was the official celebration that marked the end of the French revolution and the establishment of a short-lived constitutional monarchy in France. The event is commemorated in the annual celebration of Bastille Day.

[5] D. Diderot, *Encyclopédie ou dictionnaire raisonné des sciences, des arts et des métiers (Encyclopaedia, or reasoned dictionary of sciences, arts, and trades)*, Paris, 1751–80; new facsimile, Stuttgart: Bad Canstatt, 1966, entry for 'Encyclopédie'.

consciousness, to technology, embraced by Enlightenment scholars in a prefiguration of its ultimate global dominance. The Romans perceived the passage from dialectics to religion as a decline. They saw the most perfect monuments of language 'abandoned for a religious movement which they judged to be vulgar, destructive, and inimical to proper culture'.[6] This judgement could also be levelled at technology. Technology pushes humanity towards 'primitiveness and materiality'. It is because of this that technologies spread so effectively across vast geographical areas. A system which functions according to simple codes is easily disseminated. What is lost in terms of subtlety is gained in universality.[7]

This universalizing mentality is characteristic of the Enlightenment scholars. Simondon makes the *Encyclopaedia* the symbol of mature, or 'adult'[8] technology. He does not choose the steam-engine to represent the birth of a new system of technology. Technology's coming of age is not heralded by a new invention. It is announced by a book written by philosophers. This choice is telling: it expresses the fact that technologies outlive their technicians and that they are ultimately dependent upon the discourse that emerges concerning them. The Age of Enlightenment did not see the invention of new machines. Famous examples, like the stocking frame[9] or the fire pump, cannot obscure the fact that the technologies described in the *Encyclopaedia* had already been in use for centuries. The articles on clock makers, coopers or carpenters could have been written many

---

[6] G. Simondon, 'Les limites du progrès humain', in the journal *Revue de Métaphysique et de Morale*, 1959, vol. 3, pp. 370–6, reprinted in G. *Simondon. Une Pensée de l'individuation et de la technique*, Paris: Albin Michel, 1994, p. 272.

[7] 'Only technology can be made truly universal, because the human element that resonates within it is so primitive, so close to the basic conditions of life, that every man possesses it within himself' (*idem.*). The phrase 'Every man possesses it within himself' ('Tout homme le possède en soi') recalls Descartes' statement concerning the universality of human reason.

[8] *Mode d'existence*, p. 94.

[9] Translator's note: the stocking frame (*machine à bas*) was an early knitting machine, originally invented by William Lee of Calverton, England in 1589.

years earlier. The revolutionary nature of the *Encyclopaedia* does not derive from the information it contains, but from the fact that some of the greatest minds of the century were writing about topics with which they were not familiar. The fact that they felt called to do so, and that they heeded this call, attests to their singular mind-set.

The encyclopaedists displayed a thirst for knowledge. Their goal was to enlarge the sphere of human understanding. An encyclopaedia informs its readers of the limits of knowledge in a given domain: in so doing, it seeks to inspire others to go beyond those limits; it spurs invention. This openness distinguishes the encyclopaedia from the dictionary, which is static and fixed. Dictionaries, the product of a closed society, sanction 'correct' usage and 'proper' speech. They provide a knowledge of words, whereas the encyclopaedia describes processes that can be replicated. It is an instrument of power. According to Simondon, this book became a symbol of human mastery over nature, and the extraction of its secrets. The book is 'magic'.[10] It contains the formula for efficacious action. The emperors of antiquity were depicted holding a globe in one hand as a sign of their sovereignty. The encyclopaedists had a book: it was the intermediary through which they expressed their mastery and possession of nature.

The encyclopaedists observed the gestures of the craftsmen at work and recorded them in pictorial form, in order to facilitate their diffusion. The *Encyclopaedia* is famous for its *plates*. Images are often better suited to the task of communicating technical information than are words. Simondon alludes to this in his discussion of the geographical plates created by the Greek philosopher Thales and widely diffused among sailors of the time:

> A simple block of wood, carved with incisions that depict the contours of the coast and the places where rivers meet the sea, is worth more

---

[10] *Mode d'existence*, p. 95.

to the navigator than any poetic theogony; because this plate, a symbolic representation, integrates an accumulation of knowledge; in the course of successive voyages, it can receive new details, inserted among the earlier ones, and can be extended to include coastlines not previously explored.[11]

But this mode of communication poses a problem: the image is multivocal. The most important details are not necessarily the most salient; there is no means for calling out the features its makers wish to emphasize. The makers of the Encyclopaedia also encountered this problem. They resolved it through the use of a graphical device: hands. In numerous plates, next to an artisan at work, a disembodied hand points to whatever is most notable in the image. Floating hands indicate the steps of an operation. They represent the presence of the Encylopaedists in the world. These hands probably did not attract much attention at the time of the Encyclopaedia: they were understood in their primary function: as indicators. But today, when the illustrations are themselves historical relics, these floating hands serve as the symbols of a mentality. The universe represented in these plates is a familiar one. Man has made it his own. He humanizes everything he touches and rationalizes everything he depicts. His hand is present everywhere, obsessively. Roland Barthes expresses this in the following terms:

> You can imagine the most naturally solitary, 'savage' object; be sure that man will nonetheless appear in a corner of the image; he will be considering the object, or measuring it, or surveying it, using it at least as a spectacle; take the Giant's Causeway; that mass of terrifying basalt composed by nature in Antrim, Northern Ireland, has been, so to speak, stuffed with humanity; gentlemen in tricornes, lovely ladies contemplate the horrible landscape, chatting familiarly; ... what is striking in the entire Encyclopaedia (and especially in its images) is

[11] G. Simondon, *La perception*, course from 1964 to 1965, published in the *Bulletin de Psychologie*, January 1965, p. 570 (published in 2006, *Editions de la Transparence*).

that it proposes a world without fear … the monstrous is not excluded, but in a category much more 'surrealist' than terrifying.[12]

The hands in the *Encyclopaedia*'s plates do not suggest a tentative exploration of matter; they are the organ of technical knowledge. They signify a transfer of power. Efficacity lies not in the gesture of the artisan, not in the hands that perform the action, but in the hand that indicates, the symbol of the rationalization of technical knowledge. The hand of the *Encyclopaedia* lives on: the Internet is organized around the idea of a mobile, active hand. This neo-encyclopaedism gone wild puts all knowledge within easy reach: the user has only to point and click.

The hands of the *Encyclopaedia* are more cerebral than physical. They are representatives of reason as it enters the world of technology, transforming machines into instruments of thought. Diderot perceived a kind of intellectual perfection in the stocking frame (*machine à bas*): 'It can be viewed,' he wrote, 'as a single and unique thought.'[13] From this point forward, the machine is under the power of reason. It is a series of steps, the *conclusion* of which is a pair of stockings. Reason has taken the reins of progress. The use of technologies now has intellectual and political implications. Reason has even managed to insinuate itself into a pair of women's stockings ….

An ambiguous optimism

According to the historian Bertrand Gille, progress was a concept foreign to the world of the *Encyclopaedia*.[14] The technological systems

---

[12] R. Barthes, *Les planches de l' 'Encyclopédie'* (*The plates of the Encyclopaedia*), in *Le degré zéro de l'écriture*, Paris: Seuil, 1972, pp. 89–105, p. 95. Translated by S. Sontag in *Barthes: Selected Writings*, Fontana, 1982, p. 223. Translator's note: Sontag's translation preserves an error present in the original French: the Giant's Causeway is in Northern Ireland, not Scotland (Écosse), as Barthes erroneously indicates. The passage cited above has been modified to correct the error.

[13] *Encyclopédie, op. cit.*, entry for 'Bas' ('Stockings') (The stocking-maker's trade).

[14] B. Gille, *Histoire des techniques*, La Pléiade, Paris: Gallimard, 1978, pp. 674–5.

of the time were limited, and no one was yet aware of their potential. Simondon's judgement is less categorical. The Age of Enlightenment was not marked by *discontinuous* progress: none of the inventions of the time constituted an evolutionary breakthrough. Radical changes in living conditions would not appear until the invention of the steam-engine. But there were signs of *continuous* progress. Tools and instruments were better constructed. They became easier to use and more efficient. The gears were more precisely calibrated, the metal more finely wrought. This continuous progress did not clash with established practices. It was a process of refinement that proceeded through small innovations. This, according to Simondon, was the source of the optimism, and even 'euphoria'[15] that gripped eighteenth-century France.

The article in the *Encyclopaedia* concerning progress is quite laconic:

> PROGRESS, n.m. (*Gramm.*) movement forward; the *progress* of the sun in its orbit; the *progress* of a fire; the *progress* of this root. Also used figuratively, and one speaks of *making (rapid) progress* in an art or in science.
>
> PROGRESS *bad* (*Musical term*) one speaks of music *progressing badly* when the notes proceed at intervals that are harsh and disagreeable to the ear.[16]

This second, negative connotation is reserved for music. Technological progress is viewed favourably: the amelioration of living conditions is no cause for suspicion. A century earlier, Blaise Pascal had organized the first public transit system in Paris. Placards announced that public carriages (*carosses publics*) would circulate 'for the greatest convenience and freedom of the townspeople'.[17] Pascal's restless

---

[15] *Mode d'existence*, p. 114.
[16] *Encyclopédie, op. cit.*, entry for 'industrie'.
[17] Pascal, *Les carrosses à cinq sols*, in *Oeuvres complètes*, La Pléiade, Paris: Gallimard, 1998, p. 531.

mind, quick to sense the futility of things, was nevertheless enthusiastic about this innovation. He had only one request: if the system was profitable (a single journey cost 5 sols), the proceeds were to be given to the poor.[18] Diderot was equally serene. In his view, industry had reached an optimum level of development. Its progress was 'very gentle, and violent jolts (were) not to be feared'.[19] Everything seemed to be for the best.

The Enlightenment scholars supported technology *and* a return to nature. They saw no conflict between these two attitudes: technologies were an extension of nature. In eighteenth-century France, the influence of Descartes was still strong. Descartes had conceived of the world as an enormous clock with regular movements. Matter, the progression of seasons and the human body all functioned in a mechanical fashion. Clock makers and other technicians were only imitating nature. They were not assuming the role of creator gods, and technology was no cause for a troubled conscience. Human industry followed natural movements. The optimism of the Enlightenment was buoyed by this belief: nothing indicated that technology might represent a complete departure from what had come before. This belief, however, was based on faulty reasoning. It started from the premise that nature was mechanical, then affirmed that machines imitated nature. Technology was assumed to be a logical continuation of natural evolution. This reasoning reverses cause and effect. In drawing the conclusion that nature was guided by mechanical principles, Descartes must have been inspired by the functioning of automata. He arrived at the metaphor of the 'clockwork universe' after observing the workings of a watch and transposing them to nature.[20] In this theory, machines come first. They provide a framework through which to interpret nature.

---

[18] *Cf. Notice*, ibid*em*, p. 1293.
[19] *Encyclopédie, op. cit.*, entry for 'industrie'.
[20] Cf. G. Canguilhem, 'Machine et organisme', in *La connaissance de la vie*, Paris: Vrin, 1985.

The optimism of the Enlightenment rested on strange foundations: technologies would not modify the order of nature. They were
neither instruments of combat nor a means of resistance against
it. They were an extension of it. This is why Simondon valued the
Encyclopaedia and the mentality it represents. He saw it as a happy
phase in the history of humanity. More than this, he sought a way
to affirm in his own time the idea that technology follows the
movements of nature. But what does 'nature' signify? In a study on
the idea of nature in France in the first half of the eighteenth century,
Jean Ehrard demonstrates the complexity of this question. Nature is
a flexible, elastic idea. It allows us to justify a thing and its opposite.
In the name of nature, a case can be made for sexual freedom or for
its social repression. The noble savage is characterized by some as
the natural being *par excellence*, but for others, liberalism in politics,
economics and religion epitomizes what is natural. Nature in eighteenth-century France was associated with a variety of ideas: 'law,
reason, sentiment, virtue, happiness, innocence, society, necessity,
order, liberty'.[21]

The idea of nature allows these opposites to coexist: reason
and sentiment, necessity and liberty, nature and technology. The
optimism of the era that popularized this idea is ambiguous. It is
not the untempered optimism of those who follow a single direction
or pursue a quest. It is an optimism tinged with anxiety: it seeks to
find a 'happy medium', while abandoning nothing in the process.
The aspiration towards a more natural way of life is not at odds with
the forces of civilization. These two directions can be reconciled.
Diderot, for example, sought a middle ground between the state of
untamed nature and 'our marvelous police state'. This happy medium
would, according to Diderot, 'slow the progress of the offspring of

---

[21] J. Ehrard, *L'idée de nature en France dans la première moitié du XVIII* siècle*, Paris: Albin
     Michel, 1994 (1st edn 1963), p. 790.

Prometheus, protecting him from the Vulture and centering civilized man between the childhood of the savage and our own decrepitude.'[22] Elsewhere, he noted that the vulgar Scythians were happier than the cultivated Greeks. He suspected that a difference in intelligence was the cause, but since this was itself natural, he could not reach a definitive conclusion.

Simondon was a child of the Enlightenment scholars in two senses. He inherited their positive attitude towards technology, and he inherited their ambiguous optimism. His entire philosophy strives to reconcile opposites. He sought a 'happy medium' that could accommodate all directions, abandoning none. He salutes the Enlightenment thinkers for their humanism, which liberated people from the structures of traditional society, and he calls for a new humanism for our times. It is again necessary to free mankind, he says: while we were once liberated by our technologies, we are now, two centuries later, their slaves. He outlines a catastrophic portrait of the impact of technologies on his own era. He sees humanity as isolated, reduced to servitude. The universe is huge, our actions small and ineffectual. The vision is Pascalian: there is a feeling of emptiness. Simondon was writing fourteen years after the concentration camps and Hiroshima, five years after the death of Stalin. He evokes the 'limitless, dizzying vastness' of modern society. Technology has created a new world; all the old landmarks have been forgotten.

This assessment might lead to any number of coping strategies: political action, escape to an island, dejection, technical anarchism, poetry, asceticism. But Simondon's humanism follows a different path. He is optimistic: the problems generated by technology can be resolved by technology, and by a change of mind-set. He is also ambiguous. Like the Enlightenment philosophers, he wants to reconcile contrary ideas. It is not, however, the *idea of nature* that

---

[22] Diderot, *Réfutation de l'ouvrage d'Helvétius*, cited by Ehrard, p. 782.

provides him with the conceptual flexibility necessary to reconcile the irreconcilable. It is the *idea of technology*. He wants to preserve the mentality of the artisan while pursuing industrialization. An ecologist ahead of his time, he is also in favour of nuclear energy. He is wary of the idea of community, and yet he looks to technology as a source of new relationships. A scholarly term describes the union of opposites: *enantiodromia*, from the Greek ἐνάντιος (*enantios*), 'opposite'. It is an appropriate label for the difficult path trodden by this Encyclopaedist philosophy. Its ideal is to abandon nothing, to include everything within its ambit.

3

Marx and Simondon: Alienation

The clamour of technologies

The optimism of the Enlightenment philosophers came to an end in the nineteenth century. This century saw the appearance of 'technical individuals': tools, previously wielded by people, were now conjoined with engines, usually steam-engines. These 'individuals' were a source of malaise for human beings. There was no perceptible frustration associated with the replacement of animals by machines, but humans were profoundly affected when they themselves were displaced from their role as bearers of tools. Automatic looms, forging presses and other new factory equipment were seen as rivals, and workers destroyed them in popular uprisings.

The term 'technical elements' refers to tools and instruments. Tools (e.g. the hammer, the spear or the pen) exert an action on the world, while instruments (e.g. microscopes, stethoscopes or underwater probes) refine perception. The tool requires an energy source, while the instrument must be integrated with a structure capable of decoding the information it provides. Tools and instruments are extensions of the human body: the body acts as a source of energy or decoder of information. With the appearance of technical individuals, the human body loses pride of place.

Technical elements are now coupled with a mechanical motor. This is the case, for instance, with riveting machines, which appeared in the mid-nineteenth century. Before this, boiler makers assembled metal girders by manually hammering in rivets. The increasingly widespread use of this 'atom' of the industrial process (2.5 million rivets were used in the construction of the Eiffel Tower) led to the invention of machines for putting rivets in place. Riveting machines, powered first by steam, then by pneumatics and finally by hydraulics, are technical individuals in that they join an energy source to a hammer. Man now serves the machine. He keeps its energy source fuelled and steers it into position. The disproportion between the worker's body and the configuration of the machine is significant. It corresponds to the difference between muscular energy and the power of the steam which the body must master and whose negative effects it must avoid ('boiler's sickness' was another name for deafness). The instinctive discernment and pride of the artisan who masterfully manipulated carefully honed tools are lost when the technical individual replaces the human being. The test of courage is no longer the struggle with nature. Instead, it is the encounter with the machine.

There was no more penetrating observer of this transformation than Karl Marx. Cited several times in Simondon's work, Marx was one of the sources Simondon drew upon in his analysis of the nineteenth century. It was Marx, in fact, who first detected the transformation in the use of the human body brought about by the industrial mode of production. 'The machine tool,' he writes in Chapter 15 of *Capital*, is 'a mechanism which, having received comfortable room for manouevre, executes with its instruments the same operations previously performed by the worker with the same instruments.' Marx also took a stand in the debate in nineteenth-century France between the cinematic school and the functionalist school. The cinematic school, represented by Monge, emphasized the way in which machines transformed movement through a series of mechanisms. The functionalist school, on the other hand, characterized the machine as an ensemble of organs, each with its own function. Representatives of functionalism included Borg, Nis, Coriolis and Poncelet.[1] Marx sided with the functionalists in that he distinguished between three parts of the machine (motor force, transmission and operational components). This distinction forms the basis for his analysis of the industrialization process. The operational component was the first to be mechanized, followed by the mechanization of the power source, which corresponded to the replacement of the worker with another force (animals, wind power or hydraulics). With the advent of the steam-engine, man is deprived of his role as power source. This corresponds to the full development of the industrialization process.[2]

Simondon shared with Marx a critical attitude towards the division of labour. In his conclusion of *The Mode of Existence of Technical Objects,* he called for a profound reform of labour practices. Nevertheless, his reasons for criticizing this division of labour differed considerably from those of Marx. Having come close to the author of *Capital* in his description of alienation, Simondon's analysis ultimately moves in a different direction. A passage which initially appears Marxist in tone actually establishes the distance between them:

> It is not, essentially, the difference in scale that distinguishes the factory from the artisan's workshop, but the changed relationship between the technical object and the human being: the factory is a technical ensemble that includes automatic machines whose activities parallel those of human workers: the factory utilizes genuine technical

---

[1] Cf. J-P Séris, *La technique,* Paris: P.U.F., 1994, pp. 163–80.
[2] 'To develop the machine in all of its dimensions and the number of machine operated tools to its fullest extent requires a power source and the ability to constrain and control this force in the shape of a motor, a power source superior to the human body, without which the human is imperfect in the production of a continuous and uniform movement. Once the tool is replaced by a machine that is only guided by a man it becomes necessary to replace the human power source with other natural forces.' K. Marx (trans. B. Fowkes), *Capital,* London: Penguin, 1976, p. 492.

individuals, while in the workshop it is the human being who lends his individuality to the accomplishment of technical activities.[3]

This passage seems, at first glance, to be taking a Marxist line, but it actually contains a radical challenge to Marx's analysis. Marx considers the passage from the craftsman's workshop to machine manufacture and then to factory production as the point of emergence of the capitalist division of labour. In Chapter 14 of *Capital*, entitled 'The division of labour and manufacture', he explains that manufacturing began with the gathering of multiple independent artisanal workers in a single place. The making of a carriage, for example, required 'wheelwrights, harness-makers, tailors, locksmiths, upholsterers, turners, fringe-makers, glaziers, painters, polishers, gilders, etc.'[4] So far, this is still a matter of simple cooperation. But soon, Marx shows us that the upholsterer and the harnessmaker lose the special habits and 'turns of hand' that characterized their individual crafts: each is limited to the production of a single part of the carriage. They become specialists in a process specific to the manufacture of carriages. At this stage, Marx observes the first effects of the division of labour on the individual:

> It is not only the work that is divided, subdivided and redistributed amongst diverse individuals, but the individual himself is divided up, and transformed into the automatic motor of a detail operation, thus realizing the absurd fable of Menenius Agrippa, which presents a man as a mere fragment of his own body.[5]

Manufacture was the point of departure for the industrial revolution. It was soon superseded by the factory, which gave greater priority to mechanical production, replacing human-powered tools and machines with motor-powered machine tools. A new mode of

---

[3] *Mode d'existence*, p. 116.
[4] K. Marx, *Capital*, op. cit., p. 455.
[5] *Idem*, pp. 481–2. First line modified.

continuous mechanical production appeared. Different machine tools were combined to form an ensemble, all fed by the same power source. This central machine imposed its own rhythms on the production process, and workers were obliged to adapt. The process by which materials passed from one phase of production to the next was itself mechanized. The factory formed a coordinated whole with a single rhythm. 'In manufacture, the *isolation* of each special process is a condition imposed by the division of labour,' wrote Marx, 'whereas in the fully developed factory the *continuity* of the special processes is the regulating principle'.[6]

Simondon and Marx use identical terms. Both recognize that in the passage from the workshop to the factory, the ordering of 'who serves who? (*qui sert qui?*)' becomes inverted. In manufacture, the worker controls and is served by (*se sert de*) his tools; in the factory he serves (*sert*) the machine. Nevertheless, having acknowledged the validity of Marx's observations, Simondon proceeds to take his own analysis in a direction that places it well outside the realm of Marxist thought. He takes note of the fact that the position of factory workers prevents them from positively identifying with technical progress: when man serves machine 'the notion of progress splits in two, becomes frightening and aggressive, ambivalent'.[7] Marx's analysis moves in a circle. Having described how the worker becomes a servant of the machine, Marx takes up his analysis from the beginning, to show that through the machine the worker becomes the servant of capital, which alienates him from his labour. The relationships of servitude are doubled. They concern first the human-machine system, then the appropriation of this system in the evolution of capital. 'It is the worker,' comments Axelos, 'who, through his alienated labour, "produces" capital, and it is capital which transforms the human being into a worker, reducing

---

[6] *Idem*, p. 502. Emphasis added.
[7] *Mode d'existence*, p. 116.

him to being no more than a worker.'[8] For Marx, capital constitutes both the driving force and the final goal of the transformation from artisan's workshop to factory. Mechanization, he explained, was developed with the sole objective of augmenting relative surplus value.

Simondon rejected this idea of a double alienation to capital and to labour. Instead, and in stark contrast to the Marxist approach, he retained his focus on the relation between the human and the machine. Alienation resides at this level; it is not necessary to leave the domain of technology to locate the source of this system of slavery. 'This alienation seized upon by Marxism as having its source in the relation of the worker to the mode of production,' he writes, 'does not, in our opinion, derive solely from a relation of ownership or non-ownership between the worker and his working tools.'[9] *A more profound and more essential dimension is responsible for the alienation of the worker.* This dimension is neither legal, nor economic, nor political. *It is technological.* It concerns the 'continuity between the human individual and the technical individual, or the discontinuity between them'.[10] Continuity here refers to the successful coupling of the schematic corporeality of man and machine, while discontinuity signifies the rupture of this union. This experience is more profound than Marx's dialectics of labour, because the psycho-physiological constitution of the individual is more primal than the individual's socio-economic circumstances.

Simondon is the philosopher of technical mediation. For him, it is central. The concept of technical mediation allows Simondon to reformulate the Marxist dialectic between worker and capital, such that neither party emerges victorious. If, for Marx, the worker is alienated by capital, for Simondon, labour and capital are each

[8] K. Axelos, *Marx, penseur de la technique*, Paris: Minuit, 1961, vol. 1, p. 131.
[9] *Mode d'existence*, p. 117.
[10] *Idem*, p. 118.

alienated by their relation to technological mediation. There is no need, he writes, 'to suppose a master–slave dialectic to account for the existence of alienation within the proprietary classes (*classes possédantes*).'[11] The proprietors are just as alienated as the classes they exploit, because of their own role in relation to the machine. Whereas Marx accounts only indirectly for the alienation of the proprietary classes, through a Hegelian 'work of the negative', Simondon takes a direct, schematic approach, focused on levels of communication. He controverts Marx's reliance on the negative in favour of a higher order analysis of communication and technical mediation. For Simondon, the proprietor is alienated 'in relation to the technical object.'[12] Industrial organization distances him from the central activities of production, so that he can only reclaim his relationship with technology by means of an abstract representation of the profit derived from it. His alienation, moreover, mirrors that of the worker. 'Capital and labour are two modes of being which are equally incomplete in terms of their relation to the technical object. ... What capital has is not what labour lacks, and what capital lacks is not what labour has.'[13]

It was an act of daring to defend such a position among the intellectuals of 1950s France. But as Muriel Combes astutely notes, Simondon 'consistently denounces the alienation of human beings *in general*. ... Thus, the bankers are said to be "just as alienated in relation to the machine as the members of the new proletariat."'[14] The difficulty of Simondon's position is that it only takes individual situations into account in terms of their relation to technology, and not on their own terms. From a Simondonian point of view, conflicts and alienation are always caused by a misunderstanding of technology.

[11] *Idem.*
[12] *Idem.*
[13] *Idem.*
[14] Muriel Combes, *Simondon, Individu et collectivité*, Paris: P.U.F., 1999, p. 122.

The extreme difficulty and even 'unrealism' of this position are evident in practice. How can we conceptualize the situation in terms of the technical object and the communicative possibilities it presents, when so much else is lacking? 'Simondon,' writes Combes, 'doesn't recognize that the perspective of the workers on machines has any value. At no point does he ask himself if workers' violent hostility to machines might express something about their relationship to technology, other than mere short-sightedness.'[15] Combes elaborates on this position, pointing out that the Luddite movement in England between 1811 and 1817 has often been viewed as a negative reaction on the part of ignorant workers to the introduction of industrial machinery. But a more precise analysis of this movement reveals that it was never opposed to technology *in general*: these people were workers, and they had a practical experience of technology. Their rejection of the new system of production was a targeted response to the systematic negation of their traditional rights: the protection of women and children, guaranteed wages, and the right to organize themselves into cooperatives. From this perspective, the 'misunderstanding' denounced by Simondon appears more like clear-sighted prescience. Combes concludes:

> It is difficult to understand why, even as he deplored the fact that in labour, the machine was understood only as a means to an end, Simondon never took into account the specific experience of technology that followed from this fact. In this experience, it was not as a *man* that the worker entered the factory but as part of a mutilated humanity.[16]

---

[15] *Idem*, p. 123.
[16] *Idem*, p. 125.

Social utopia and economy

Simondon's position seems, on the basis of this discussion, to be far removed from concrete situations. Critics of Marx are as numerous as Marxists. But never, to our knowledge, has anyone refuted him in the name of technology. Not technology as a source of profit, a means of transforming the world, or an instrument of power, but pure technology: something that demands to be known, respected and understood. The technical object has become the measure of all things. It serves as a reference point against which we can evaluate the alienation of rich and poor. What is surprising, given Simondon's general views on the topic, is that technology, which he uses to discredit the exploited and the exploiter alike, is at first merely a means. Although neutral at the outset, technical mediation assumes such proportions in Simondon's philosophy that it acquires the power to adjudicate in matters of human alienation. The result of this is even more surprising. If we follow his reasoning to its logical conclusion, we discover a system in which alienation no longer exists. In this vision of the future, technology is respected; humans have learned how to 'communicate well' with technology: that is, to communicate on its level and not theirs. One thinks of Huxley's *Brave New World*....

And yet this 'unrealism' resonates. It is increasingly acknowledged that the development of technology has become an end in itself. In certain activities, technology is now the regulator of social relations and bestower of responsibilities. Might Simondon's 'unrealism' be a prophecy? He envisaged a system in which communism and capitalism would both be outmoded; a technical system in which our current conceptions of what it means to be human would no longer apply. Simondon joins Nietzsche, Foucault and Bataille in proclaiming the 'death of man'. But for Simondon it is not the will to power, irrationality or desire that has dethroned the 'political animal'. It is technology.

Simondon was an opponent of technocracy. The technocrats turned progress into an idea, distancing themselves from material relations. Technocracy is an intellectual projection. Saint-Simonism serves as a prime example of this. Saint-Simon wanted to reorganize society by making labour the basis of all social hierarchy. He proscribed idleness and would only admit the productive into his new society. The only aristocracy he would countenance was one of scientists, artists and workers. He sought to unite their efforts around a single goal. He wanted to redistribute social resources and establish new foundations for the organization of religion, the family and property. Saint-Simon was a technocrat *avant la lettre*, a 'functionary of ideas' who wanted to implement his doctrine. In Simondon's view, the implementation of such a programme could only be achieved by using technology to drive a wedge between concrete perceptions and abstract projections. Thus liberated, these projections become 'technocratic and enslaving'.[17] Concentrated exclusively on the level of the technical *ensemble*, they are no longer moderated by matter or gesture. Technocracy is an unbridled will to conquest.

> This conquering aggression has the character of an assault on nature. Mankind gains possession of the earth, penetrating it, crossing and ploughing it over, breaking through barriers which until that day had remained impassable. There is in technocracy a certain sense of violation of the sacred.[18]

Technocracy is prideful and demiurgic, animated by a will to power that nothing holds in check, because it has been intellectualized. Alienation, for Simondon, is rooted in this intellectualism, which has the knowledge and the idea of power (*puissance*) while lacking any concrete power (*pouvoir*), except for that which it appropriates from others for its own purposes. 'The technocrats in France are

---

[17] *Idem*, p. 127.
[18] *Idem*.

predominantly "polytechnicians",[19] men who, in their understanding of technology, are in the position of "advanced users" and organizers rather than true technicians.[20]

Simondon is as much a critic of economics as he is of technocracy. The desire to move beyond economics is at the root of his critique of Marx. This attitude has its precedent in one of the earliest legends of Western philosophy. It is recounted that Thales (sixth century BC) was derided for his poverty, and for the uselessness of philosophy, since it had failed to bring him wealth. So, Thales studied the sky and predicted that there would be an excellent olive harvest. He got together some capital and acquired rights on all the olive presses in Miletus and Chios. He turned an enormous profit, demonstrating that philosophers could enrich themselves if they chose, but that this goal was of no interest to them. Simondon subscribed to this myth. His critique of Marx was not that of a capitalist. It was motivated more by a rejection of the cult of economy and by the idea that technologies had a more profound impact on society than did economics.

On more than one occasion, Simondon attacked the 'ethics of returns' (*morale du rendement*), the framing of moral decisions in terms of economic pay-offs. He wished for a change of mentality concerning consumption, the commercialization of objects, and utilitarianism. The new mentality would be characterized by a respect for labour as the source of value in each object and an intuitive appreciation of the natural and technological cycles at the origin of

---

[19] Translator's note: Simondon uses the term *polytechniciens*, which in French refers to graduates of the École Polytechnique, the most prestigious engineering school in France, who have historically entered positions of influence in government, industry, research and finance. Simondon seems to be applying the label more broadly here, to establish a pointed contrast between the 'polytechnicien' and the true 'technicien'.

[20] *Idem*, pp. 127–8. Simondon's thinking here aligns with that of François Châtelet. In a chapter entitled 'Pour le plaisir de la définition' ('For the pleasure of definition') Châtelet writes that the problem of technocracy is not that it reifies man but that it is 'without a concept'. 'This is to say that technocracy is an ideology.' He also affirms the 'truth' of the technician in contrast with the technocrat who seeks to be 'the technician of a science that does not exist'. Cf. F. Châtelet, *Questions. Objections*, Paris: Denoël, 1979, p.143.

any production process.[21] He called for resistance to the culture of consumerism that he saw developing:

> An ethics of returns is forming which will constitute a new species of communitarian ethics.... It is not because a civilization loves money that it attaches itself to an ethics of returns; rather, it is because a civilization is based on returns that it becomes a civilization based on money.... Despite civil liberties, it is restrictive for individuals.[22]

But how can technological development be separated from the ethics of returns? Marx converted the question of technology into one of economics. For him, the idea of a philosophy of technology detached from the context of socio-political problems is unthinkable. This is

---

[21] In his seminal course on the psycho-sociology of technology (*Psycho-sociologie de la technicité*), printed in the *Bulletin de l'École pratique de Psychologie et de Pédagogie de Lyon, 1960–61,* Simondon identifies a type of alienation distinct from that of either Feuerbach, whose focus is the separation between man and the sacred, or that of Marx. This third type of alienation is produced by the liberation of the technical object when it detaches itself from its producer and goes to market, with no specific user in mind. 'When an artisan,' he writes, 'constructs an object for use in his workshop, or when an artisan builds something for a specific customer, there is no alienation, because the object is never detached from its producer or its ultimate user. But in industrial production, the distance between production and use increases: the object is produced without a clearly defined conception of how it will be used' (p. 228). Simondon sees in this a virtualization of human labour. But the premise of this analysis is not beyond critique. One counter-example would be the situation of writers, who also send their products 'to market' and accept the distance that separates them from their eventual readers, sometimes by a period of centuries. This separation does not signify that their work is virtualized. Virtualization concerns, above all, the standardization of objects and the grafting on of superfluous and inessential features. Baudrillard, whose discussion of the sociology of consumption builds upon Simondon's analysis, expresses this as follows: 'There is a cancer of the object: the proliferation of astructural elements that underpins the object's triumphalism is a kind of cancer. It is upon such astructural elements (automatism, accessory features, inessential differences) that the entire social network of fashion and controlled consumption is founded. They are the bulwark that tends to halt genuine technical development. On their account, while appearing to manifest all the metamorphic powers of a prodigious health, objects that are already saturated wear themselves out completely through convulsive formal variation and changes whose impact is strictly visual'. (Cf. J. Baudrillard (trans. James Benedict), *System of Objects,* London: Verso, 2005, p. 134). Baudrillard's critique of Simondon is summed up in this observation: 'But it is clear that, for reckoning with the *quotidian* system of objects, this technological and structural analysis is deficient.' This criticism should not go unchallenged. Simondon adds much to our understanding of quotidian objects, notably through his 'techno-aesthetic'. This aspect of his philosophy will be further explored in the third part of this book.

[22] G. Simondon, *L'individuation psychique et collective,* Paris: Aubier, 1989, p. 289.

the source of Simondon's discontentment with Marxism. Simondon does not deny the relationship between economy and technology, but he advocates for something different: *a technology that is not centred on consumption and returns, a technology that cannot be reduced to questions of profit.* His anti-Marxism rests on the idea that technological progress is too profound to be limited to the commercial sphere. It is capable of changing mentalities, perceptions, ways of life, and even the human body. It carries the seeds of a 'new' humanity. The economic sphere, short-sighted and riveted to the present situation, cannot claim, according to Simondon, to exercise authority over situations that lie beyond its scope.

Evolutionary logic

To understand Simondon's argument, we must position it within a logic of evolution. Etymologically, economics relates to habitat.[23] It is first and foremost a way of managing the present. The accumulation of wealth is only a driving force of human development (*devenir*) in the short term. Technology, in contrast, is a vector of radical transformation, of humanity and of the world. It can change the course of evolution. A philosophy that seeks to fully engage with technology cannot relegate it to the realm of economic considerations, be they Marxist or capitalist.

The driving force of Simondon's critique is ontological. This is both its strength and its weakness. Its strength, because it makes clear the ways in which technological progress relativizes the traditional conception of an unchangeable 'human nature'. The possibilities opened up by technological evolution are incommensurate with

---

[23] Translator's note: From the Ancient Greek οἰκονομία (*oikonomia*), 'management of the household'; from οἶκος (oikos), 'house' and νόμος (nomos), 'custom or law'.

the problems of day-to-day consumption, the use of gadgets or the feelings of power derived from owning a luxury car. The question of becoming (*devenir*) as it pertains to humanity is of a different stature from questions of commerce. But this perspective is not without equally significant weaknesses. By making the question of technology purely ontological, by setting aside all secondary considerations and looking always towards the future, Simondon has a tendency to forget what technologies are in reality. A technology that did not engage in any way with capital or consumption would soon dwindle to nothing. In his course on the psycho-sociology of technology (*Psycho-sociologie de la technicité*), Simondon contrasts the 'vulgarity or absurdity of consumer goods'[24] with the majesty of a satellite launching. The significance of this gesture is real, but it is economic as much as it is technological. Oil contracts, lobbying by suppliers, the salaries of technicians, the power of the military industrial complex in the country that launches the satellite, the financial consequences for the telecommunications industry (sometimes eliciting negative backlash) indicate that this technological gesture fits tightly within a socio-economic network. A satellite's orbit around the earth has as many financial consequences as the turning of a roulette wheel at a casino.

Simondon's ontology thus reveals itself to be 'abstract' in the Marxist sense of the term: unwilling to acknowledge the relations of production. However, Simondon's ontology is also a critique. He is engaging in wishful thinking, anticipating a time when economics will loosen its stranglehold on technology. In so doing, he signals his conviction that the system has gone astray. The market appropriates technologies and re-fashions them into instruments of profit. This analysis applies to numerous cases: the histories of information technology, aviation or cell phones all culminate in the appropriation

---

[24] *Psycho-sociologie de la technicité, op. cit.,* p. 344.

of these technologies by those who seek to exploit them commercially, at any price. However, even prior to their commercial reappropriation, these inventions were not 'pure' products of technological progress. All of them were originally developed for military purposes. Networked technologies came into being due to the need to decentralize command posts in case of enemy bombardment. Progress in our understanding of atoms and of bacterial populations also came about through military research. The 'war effort' was a collaboration involving military, technological, economic and social sectors.

Marx is certainly right on this count: there is no technology that is not shaped by ulterior interests. But Simondon's analysis remains relevant as the expression of a point of view that is intentionally radical. By setting aside what appear to be the central questions, he uncovers the underlying currents that guide technological progress, which these questions often obscure from view.

4

Cybernetics

Information: Relations between *alter technos*

Around 1940, a new discipline emerged: information science. It was the work of mathematicians, logicians, engineers, linguists and biologists. For the most part, these scholars grouped themselves under the theoretical banner of cybernetics, a neologism based on the Greek word κυβερνήτης (kubernétes), meaning 'one who steers or governs'. Its founder, the American mathematician Norbert Wiener, defined cybernetics as 'the study of control and communication in the (human) animal and the machine'. The goal of this transdisciplinary theory was to promote the transmission of information and the control of action.

Cybernetics presents information as the theoretical foundation of the classical disciplines. The transmission of information is a phenomenon that underpins biology, electronics and psychology. Examples include the biological processes of hormonal regulation within the body and electronic devices ranging from the tube lamp to cutting-edge applications of nanotechnology. Starting in the 1940s, scientists began to redefine certain theoretical areas of their disciplines using terms borrowed from information science. In addition to a shared vocabulary, cyberneticists also gained a scientific method of analysis that guaranteed precision. This project came with one disqualifying principle: any terms judged to be vague or imprecise were banished and replaced with univocal information functions. In Wiener's view, words, like 'life', 'purpose' and 'soul' were essentially useless for scientific thought. This movement towards the refinement of natural language into a new, more precise means of communication was accompanied by a directive to all disciplines: concepts should be expressed in operational terms. 'Control', 'command', 'communicate', 'move', 'act' and 'react' were the verbs favoured by proponents of cybernetics, since they lent themselves to technical schematization. Cybernetics is both theoretical and practical. It was, perhaps, the first intentionally techno-scientific enterprise, where to theorize a phenomenon was to modify it. Wiener's professional path led him towards this synthesis. He formulated the principles of cybernetics as a result of his research into missile technology. During the Second World War, the American government assigned him the task of developing a device capable of automatically aiming and firing an anti-aircraft missile launcher: the goal was to locate the target aircraft, then aim for a location further along in its trajectory. The device guiding the missile launcher would have to react to the speed and location of the plane and use this information to aim accordingly at its future location, a retroactive process which Wiener successfully developed in 1942, giving it the name of 'feed-back'. He would later speak of a symmetrical 'feed-forward' mechanism.

Cybernetics seemed to be the product of a futuristic imagination. Specialist magazines of the period feature photographs of scientists in white coats, working on communication machines: railway network control centres, punch card readers, electroencephalograms, telephone exchange switchboards, etc. Cybernetics insisted on connections and automatic channels, in which each machine sequences its tasks in response to signals received from the previous machine in the chain. The technical object was no longer alone. Cables and electric wires connected it to an associated environment, also controlled by technology. The evocative power of these photographs comes, above all, from what they fail to show, because there is no way for them to show it: relay technologies, the *alter techno* with which the machines communicated; for example, signal switches, elsewhere in the country, whose position could be modified in response to feedback from the input device. The ambience in these photographs is calm, confident. Cybernetics had turned control into a positive attribute. This new concept of control no longer concerned energy, which had fuelled the industries of the nineteenth century, but rather, information. The smoking locomotive, whose arrival at the station had been immortalized, through different media, by Zola and the Lumière brothers, was now succeeded by the image of a railway network dispatching centre. This shift of focus shows that the original technical stakes were no longer in play. The rails had been laid, the trains were running. Cybernetics signalled that progress would now take place in the intimacy of a control room, where the material operators were represented and controlled at a distance.

Simondon was among the first to bring cybernetics to France. He read Wiener's writings as soon as they were published. Simondon shared Wiener's enthusiasm for a transdisciplinary theory organized around mutually agreed-upon concepts. He described phenomena using operational terms and adopted the vocabulary of the cyberneticists, with recurring references to communication, control, relations, functions, actions and reactions. He was, however, more wary of the social and political aspects of cybernetics. He rejected the myth of the 'human-machine' hybrid, the possibility of rationalizing human behaviour, and other oversimplified conceptualizations. Cybernetics is in some ways more notable for the enthusiasm it inspired than for the theoretical results it produced. These results, as we shall see, ultimately did not have a decisive impact. Cybernetics was, for a time, the banner and the face of progress. The epistemological revolution that Simondon attributes to it must be viewed, from a philosophical perspective, as a qualified success. Above all, it provides us with an excellent pretext to examine the 'great convergence' that spans the history of information science.

Encounters with signs, matter and memory

The enthusiasm that cybernetics generated in the 1950s was considerable. Simondon helps us to grasp one source of this enthusiasm: cybernetics represents a particular type of concretization. The concrete technical object facilitates interaction among elements emanating from different contexts. The objects explored up until this point consisted of combinations of technical elements: the locomotive, for example, united the steam-engine with infrastructures created for the mining industry. Cybernetics went beyond this material framework by integrating language. The objects that resulted from this revolution (computers, telephones, electronic control centres, information networks, etc.) were hybrids that combined material equipment with language, technology with logic. Cybernetics expanded the technical domain, integrating it with typically human instruments: signs and, in certain cases, significations.

'Information machines' are situated at the point where two philosophical traditions intersect. They mediate between a material tradition and a logical tradition. In one tradition, logical reasoning must be expressed verbally; in the other, it must be 'materialized', that is, represented visually and concretely through the use of a supporting mechanism. Aristotle, Lull, Leibniz, Bacon, Boole and Turing belong to the logical tradition. Each of them sought a formalized expression of logical reasoning. The material tradition is more empirical: the inventors of the abacus, Lull, then Pascal, Leibniz, Babbage and various engineers who have, for the most part, remained anonymous succeeded in configuring matter so that it would retain a record, or memory, of information. Cybernetics is the meeting point of these two traditions. In computer science, the operation that describes this convergence is called *implementation*. To implement is to inscribe a logical structure in material form, by programming an electronic circuit. The cybernetics craze was inspired by this convergence of the logical and the material. These two traditions did not develop independently of one another. Historically, they had already intersected more than once. Users of the abacus manipulated stone or ivory markers in space to express numerical information. The value of the markers was indicated by the position they occupied. In this way, mathematical operations were represented not by written signs or symbols, but by the material configuration of the abacus.

Raymond Lull

In the thirteenth century, Raymond Lull (or Ramón Llull, in Catalan) invented a material mechanism for expressing verbal reasoning. Born in the Majorcan city of Palma in 1235, he came late to academic study. At the age of 40, having spent his life as an adventurer, Lull turned to religion and took refuge in the study of logic and theology. He studied Aristotle, Averroes, Middle Eastern languages, and the work of Spanish alchemists. Eventually, he developed a plan to use science and knowledge as a means to convert the 'infidels' who posed a threat to Christian believers. Following on the heels of the military crusades, his was the crusade of a theoretician. He was supported by the financially ruined pope, who could no longer afford to fund another military campaign. Lull travelled twice to Tunisia, armed with his invention, the *ars magna*, intended to persuade the Muslim population to convert to Christianity. He was greeted first with indifference, then with derision. Lull attributed this reaction to the inadequacy of his machine, to which he had delegated all his powers of persuasion. He went back to Majorca to further perfect his machine, then returned to Tunisia with a more refined model. Exasperated by his insistence, his audience stoned him, and ultimately killed him.

Lull's *ars magna* was for him a means of expressing all possible combinations and permutations of thought. It contained an exhaustive formal representation of reasoning, and Lull considered it to be a comprehensive recapitulation of the philosophical thought of his time. His confidence arose from the conviction that his machine left no space for interpretation – so much so that the conversion of anyone who handled it should have been guaranteed. The device consisted of several concentric circles overlayed on one another. The top circle contained the nine subjects: *Deus, angelus, coelum, homo, imaginatiuum, sensitiuum, vegetatiuum, elementatiuum, instrumentatiuum*. The second circle contained the nine attributes: *bonitas, magnitudo, duratio, potentas, cognitio, appetitus, virtus, veritas, gloria*. Aligning the texts in each circle would produce propositions such as *Deus est magnus* or *angelus est bonus*. To these subjects and attributes, Lull added the nine modes of being: difference, concordance, conflict, beginning, middle, end, superiority, equality, inferiority. These were featured on the outermost circle.

Lull's invention was the object of much derision, notably that of Sir Francis Bacon. Giordano Bruno defended it and attempted to construct his own version; Leibniz admired it. Nonetheless, Lull's invention did not avoid the problem of faulty reasoning.[1] It could be used to construct contradictory or nonsensical arguments, such as 'Goodness presents both a great concordance and a great conflict'.

---

[1] Borges notes that 'measured against its objective, judged by its inventor's illustrious goal, the thinking machine does not work. For us, that fact is of secondary importance. The perpetual motion machines depicted in sketches that confer their mystery upon the pages of the most effusive encyclopedias don't work either, nor do the metaphysical and theological theories that customarily declare who we are and what manner of thing the world is. Their public and well-known futility does not diminish their interest. This may (I believe) also be the case with the useless thinking machine.' Borges, Jorge Luis. 'Ramón Lull's Thinking Machine' (1937), in *Selected Non-fictions*, edited by Eliot Weinberger; translated by Esther Allen, Suzanne Jill Levine and Eliot Weinberger (New York: Viking, 1999), pp. 155–9.

The historic interest of his invention is in its novelty: it succeeds in creating a spatial and dynamic representation of verbal reasoning. Not only did Lull create a material representation of verbal reasoning, a task which writing itself also accomplishes, he made the interpretation of his verbal propositions dependent upon their position in space. A change in the positioning of the circles results in a change to the proposition expressed. Lull's genius was in tying together two disparate problems: the formal representation of verbal reasoning and the modification of a spatial organization. For this reason he belongs to both traditions: that of logic and that of the configuration of matter. His invention made the intersection between the two concrete.

Leibniz

Leibniz's reflections on language and classification represent a turning point in the process of organizing and formalizing verbal reasoning. Leibniz shared with other classical thinkers the determination to find a rigorous formula for analysing language. He chose to take the most basic elements as his point of departure. This idea, already present in Lull's philosophy, would resurface in the works of Bacon, Locke and Descartes.[2] Leibniz's work contains numerous reflections on signs and their relationship to *things*. A sign is 'that which we perceive in this moment, but which we also judge to be connected to something

---

[2] In a letter to Mersenne, Descartes wrote on this subject, 'I believe that it would be possible to invent the words and written characters of a language that could be learnt very quickly. Order is what is needed: all the thoughts which can come into the human mind must be arranged in an order like the natural order of the numbers. In a single day one can learn to name every one of the infinite series of numbers, and thus to write infinitely many different words in an unknown language. The same could be done for all the other words necessary to express all the other things which fall within the purview of the human mind. ... But *the invention of such a language* depends upon true philosophy. For without that philosophy it is impossible to number and order all the thoughts of men' (Descartes, 20 November 1629, in *Descartes: Philosophical Letters*, translated and edited by Anthony Kenny, Oxford: Clarendon Press, 1970, pp. 3–6, edits to translation by Aliza Krefetz).

else, as a result of an anterior experience, either our own, or that of someone else'.[3] The sign is relational: it establishes a link between the subject and the world of experience, real or imagined.

Leibniz sought to refine the role of signs in the transmission of knowledge. He reflected on the nature of memory and of invention. Many of his professional pursuits led him to consider questions of mnemonics. As a young man, he attempted to bring order to the judicial system of his age, which he characterized as '*infinitum, incertum, arbitrarium*'. Convinced that the system was regressing into chaos, he strove to create a system of organization that would facilitate searches for specific judicial decisions and documents. Later, while serving as librarian at the ducal libraries of Wolffenbüttel and Hanover, he was again confronted with problems of organization and inventory. His first written works on systems of classification concerned the arrangement of libraries. His activities as the official genealogist for the House of Brunswick led him to address further questions of organization. Searches for documents, classification of library holdings and the construction of family trees necessitated a formalized language. Aside from these practical concerns, Leibniz's metaphysical studies also called for the ability to operate on multiple planes. Leibniz multiplied perspectives on things, demonstrating that each discrete item belonged to multiple classes. Indexes, catalogues, inventories and directories were the focus of his thoughts. From these preoccupations emerged questions of how to memorize and store information (*ars retendi*) and how to retrieve information that had been committed to memory (*ars revocandi* or *ars reminiscendi*). He was sensitive to the need for economy: memory is limited. To avoid overtaxing it, it was necessary to find systems of signs that were at once as simple and as evocative as possible.

Leibniz criticized natural language for its arbitrariness. The connection between a sign and the memory it evokes is not

---

[3] M. Dascal, *La sémiologie de Leibniz*, Paris: Aubier, 1978, p. 78.

inherent. His *universal characteristic (characteristica universalis)* was intended to overcome this flaw. It was an alphabet of human thought, a comprehensive catalogue of simple ideas, designated by signs or numeric rankings. The universal characteristic only used elements with inherent, fixed values to avoid any possible confusion about the signification of the signs. It was an algebra of human thought.

Practically speaking, the mnemonic function of the signs depended on their spatial organization. Perceiving a specific arrangement of signs would elicit a specific memory. Systems of signs would be so efficient that they could bypass the thing being represented 'to follow the very idea of the thing'.[4] Technical schemas, atlases, maps, musical scores and zodiac charts all accomplish this function. In the zodiac chart, the drawing of the lion's mane stands in for the lion; double signs are represented by doubled figures. The information depicted reflects the organization of the thing being represented. Like his successors, the Encyclopaedists, Leibniz was convinced that the universalization and popularization of knowledge would be brought about through schematic systems of organization.[5] The typographic symbols he invented to classify judicial rulings are one example of this. To represent opposition he would write ')('; for resemblance, '()'; for the cause, 'o-'; for the effect, '-o'; for the category, '∩' and for the sub category, 'U'.

The canonical example of the universal character is binary notation. Leibniz pointed out that it is more 'fundamental', more closely tied to the numbers it represents than classic decimal notation, which he denounced as graphically arbitrary. Whereas it is impossible

---

[4] Dascal, p. 152.
[5] 'One could' he explained in his *New Essays*, 'introduce a set of *Universal Characters* that would be very popular and superior (to those of the Chinese), by using small diagrams in place of words.... The use of this means of writing would be of great utility in enriching our imaginations and producing thoughts that are less muffled and less word-dependent than those we have at present' (Leibniz, G. W., *Nouveaux essais sur l'entendement humain* (*New Essays on Human Understanding*), 1705, Book IV, chapter vi).

to deduce that 3 x 3 = 9 is an inherent relationship, based on the graphical representation of the numbers '3' and '9', this deduction is possible from the binary representations of the numbers: '11' and '1001'. The binary characters graphically express certain properties of the numbers they designate. This is the key to their utility as a means of recording knowledge.

Pascal

In 1628, Wilhelm Schickard, a German, built the first calculating machine. In 1642, Blaise Pascal independently constructed a device which would allow his father, the tax commissioner of Upper Normandy, to perform calculations 'on the spokes of gear wheels'. His invention was called the Pascaline. For its construction he enlisted clock makers, who were, as a guild, responsible for the maintenance of mechanical regulating devices. Pascal's machine employed the decimal system. It consisted of several gear wheels, each representing a different place value within the decimal system: one wheel for the ones' place, another for the tens' place, etc. An adjustable stylus kept each wheel in the position of the digit it was to display. This digit could be read through a small window. An outer cover concealed the other digits inscribed along the wheel's circumference. A notched disc was used to turn the wheels until they displayed the desired number. Each wheel was attached to a small weight, which was lifted as the wheel turned, moving from 0 to 1, from 1 to 2, etc., until it finally passed from 9 to 0. When the counter passed to 0 the weight would fall, activating the neighbouring wheel, the marker for the tens' place, which would move up by one digit.

This was the carry mechanism. When writing out an addition or subtraction problem by hand, we indicate that a digit is to be carried from one place value to the next by marking it at the top of the neighbouring column. The genius of Pascal's invention was to mechanize this system of carrying over digits using a system of weights: each time one of the wheels made a complete revolution, the attached weight would convey this information to the neighbouring wheel. The carry mechanism served as a mechanical memory of operations. Pascal's invention of this mechanism marked a significant step forward in the mechanization of calculations. Not only did his machine connect numerical values to the position of the wheels, but its carry mechanism provided a 'materialization', a mechanical memory of each operation. Signs, memories and positions are the means by which information processing is 'materialized'. Leibniz would conceptualize this theoretically in his observation that memory was a function of the position of signs. He also put it into practice by developing a machine that could perform multiplication and division.

Turing

The British logician Allan Turing played a significant role at two different points in the history of information technology: first in 1936, as a logic theorist, and then, during the Second World War, as a leading participant in England's code-breaking operations. It was in the first of these two roles that he invented his 'universal machine'. Turing first described this hypothetical machine – an automaton operating on logical principles – in a 1936 article entitled *On Computable Numbers, with an Application to the "Entscheidungsproblem"*.[6] Turing's hypothetical machine was part of his contribution to the solution of a problem posed in 1904 by David Hilbert, a mathematician at the University of Göttingen. Hilbert wanted to establish a set of indisputable axioms which could form the basis of all of mathematics. He felt that a logical foundation of mathematics could be established

---

[6] *Proceedings of the London Mathematical Society*, Ser. 2, vol. 43, 1938, pp. 544–6.

if all mathematical propositions were considered as sets of symbols rather than as theoretical propositions. In this view, writing gains primacy over signification: the proof of a proposition or theory can be reduced to a finite series of written symbols.

Hilbert also proposed to realign mathematical logic with number theory, for which Peano's axioms provided the basic foundation. These axioms served as a framework from which the other branches of mathematics, and the most complex theorems of number theory, could be derived. The problem posed by Hilbert was one of decidability: are there any true propositions which nonetheless cannot be proven in the existing system? Since proving a proposition, according to Hilbert's stipulations, meant producing a finite series of signs which did not contradict any of the axioms, the question became a material problem of representing signs in written form. Hilbert held that all true propositions were decidable. Were this not so, his attempt to establish a foundation for mathematics would be futile. However, in 1931, Gödel demonstrated that Hilbert's belief in decidability was mistaken. He produced a proposition that was undecidable in Peano's formal arithmetic system. Gödel's proof of undecidability respected Hilbert's dictate that signs must be represented 'materially'. Gödel wrote out a finite series of signs; more precisely, he associated each symbol and each operator with a number, called a 'Gödel number'. Using this method, he could translate a proposition, or even a proof, into numbers.

Turing's 1936 article enlarged the discussion of these problems by linking decidability to calculability, or more specifically, to algorithms. An algorithm is a finite series of elementary processes, which, when followed in a routine manner produce a calculation. For example, the operation written as 3 x 8 is equivalent to the sequence 'Take the number 8. Add 8 to it and keep the result in memory. Add 8 to the remembered sum, and record this final result.' Algorithms constitute the basis of computer programming. In his article 'On computable Numbers', Turing used algorithms to address the problem of decidability. This approach radicalized Hilbert's position: Turing demonstrated that writing a proof, which Hilbert defined as a finite series of symbols, was equivalent to constructing an algorithm. A formula is decidable if it can be calculated by the universal logic machine. The criterion of decidability is directly linked to the machine's ability to function: if the machine produces a finite series of signs, the proposition is decidable. If the series produced is infinite, such that the machine never comes to a stop, the proposition must be considered undecidable. Turing thus overcame another hurdle in the process of mechanizing formal reasoning, by transforming mathematical proofs into mechanical operations carried out by a machine. In so doing, he created the blueprint for the computers of the future. Twelve years before the first electronic computer came into being, Turing's universal machine anticipated its combination of an algorithmic program, a memory (infinite, in Turing's case), a control panel, and a unit to process written inputs and generate written outputs.

Turing saw a way to bring matter and memory together. He set out the conditions by which an isomorphism could be established between two seemingly incommensurate realities. His logic constructed a bridge between them, thus enabling a transaction that was to be of increasing importance: the storage of data in material form. The role of technology was changing. It would no longer serve merely as a mediator between humankind and nature. It was to become a second memory. Books also serve as a type of external memory. But there are two essential differences between books and computer technologies. First, books are not encoded in a binary language unintelligible to most human beings. The words they display are not translated from another format; they are stored as is. Second, printed text does not change, although its interpretation may evolve over time. Computers, in contrast, operate on the data stored within them. From a subjective point of view, humankind displays an extraordinary degree of trust in its machines. For Simondon, cybernetics is a logical consequence of progress. It must be assumed that trust in machines, which is the corollary to an embrace of cybernetics, is also a logical consequence.... The *alter techno* is seen as more reliable than the *alter ego*. This is a slippery slope that leads from technology to individualism. For some, it is also an enticing slope that leads to the expansion of information science.

By way of conclusion: Discussion of two ways of representing progress

The idea of creating autonomous life by inscribing a word or symbol into matter has been the subject of fantasy since ancient times. The inscription of the word אמת (*emet*) 'truth' on the Golem's forehead brings him to life. With the removal of the *aleph* from the beginning of the word, the meaning changes to 'death': the Golem turns back into clay. Unlike the kabbalists of Prague, the cyberneticians did not rely on sacred significations. They began with the most primitive elements: *yes* or *no*, *0* or *1*. This disjunction was a reflection of the material world; it corresponds to the two possible positions of a switch, *open* or *closed*. This is the cornerstone on which the edifice of cybernetics rests.[7] It forms the groundwork for an enormous enterprise of translation. The language of cybernetics is inscribed in silicon memory chips. It is transmitted through optical fibres. It can also operate directly: joined to a motor, information machines can produce mechanical and energetic effects.

Matter and memory, which Bergson had defined as separate, were now rejoined through the intermediary of the sign. It is not

---

[7] *Cf.* A. Robinet, *Le défi cybernétique. L'automate et la pensée*, Paris: Gallimard, 1973.

surprising then that when the time came, cyberneticians turned towards metaphysics. Matter and memory; body and spirit. They had found a connection. Free from psychological hang-ups, free from the prohibitions and damnations that haunted the kabbalists. Free from the scruples of the philosophers who felt compelled to distinguish between mortal flesh and immortal spirit. In the 1950s, information theory appeared on the horizon like a promised land. After years of wandering in the desert of myth and philosophy, it established a perfect *mediation* between matter and the immaterial world. Simondon understood this. He saw the benefits that physics, biology, psychology and sociology could extract from this new technological paradigm.

Our interpretation of the present depends on whether we view the history of technology as an epic narrative or as a contingent one. The epic puts its emphasis on the broad strokes that give shape to history. In this narrative, there is a sense of movement. The abacus, Aristotle, Lull, Pascal, Leibniz, Turing, and contemporary engineers of information theory are like links in a chain, leading inexorably to the current situation. The epic model assumes that the convergence of these efforts and these inventions was not coincidental: it is guided by an unconscious force, an invisible hand, a teleological process. The compatibility of formal reasoning and material structures is too improbable to have been stumbled upon purely by chance. Philosophies of progress often take the epic approach – Hegel is a prime example. They use past events to elicit a sense of necessity or inevitability: history could not have happened differently, since everything converged to make it happen as it did.

Voltaire satirized this opinion in *Candide*. 'It is demonstrable', says Pangloss, 'that things cannot be otherwise than as they are: for, all being created for an end, all is necessarily for the best end'. Noses were made to bear spectacles. Thus, we have spectacles. The universe contains stones and stonemasons so that the Baron of

Thunder-Ten-Tronckh could live in the most magnificent castle in all of Westphalia. Everything is for the best: his castle has not only a door, but windows.

The alternative perspective is less triumphant. The contingent view of history is sensitive to the role of luck and chance, and to the infinity of potentialities contained in an infinite number of situations. This perspective insists on the singularity of each achievement. It is sceptical of teleological thinking. Contingent history is thus more mature. Like a patient undergoing psychoanalysis, it has learned that there is not one single history, but only different stories to be told about the past, which depend upon the point of view of the story-teller. It refuses to subjugate twenty-six centuries of philosophy and technology in the service of its own triumphant narrative. Students of historical contingency do not believe in the best of all possible worlds, and what others call 'progress' they see more neutrally as 'change'. They are mindful of diverging paths in the course of history. They think in terms of 'butterfly effects' and 'Cleopatra's nose', small details that change the face of the world[8] and momentous alliances, the historical significance of which is unknown to their participants.[9] Their relationship with the past inspires in them the optimism of the iconoclast: since things could have happened differently in the past, they may yet turn out differently in the future.

In the *Mode of existence of technical objects*, Simondon does not say which approach he favours. Does he take an epic view of history, or is he a relativist? He speaks neither of necessity nor of contingency.

---

[8] Translator's note: This is an allusion to Pascal's famous remark that, had Cleopatra's nose been shorter, 'the whole face of the world would have been changed' ('Le nez de Cléopâtre s'il eût été plus court, toute la face de la terre aurait changé.' Pascal, *Pensées*, p. 162).

[9] In an article on the development of computer science, Pierre Lévy talks about a 'cascade of misappropriations and reinterpretations of heterogeneous and diverse materials'. For him, there is no covert federation, no shared intention, but only individual strategies, coincidences and collisions between constraint and innovation. Cf. P. Lévy, 'L'invention de l'ordinateur' (The invention of the computer), in M. Serres (ed.), *Éléments d'histoire des sciences*, Paris: Bordas, 1989, pp. 515–35.

He seems, at times, to take a relativist stance, for example, when he refuses to consider traditional technical training 'as necessarily inferior to training that uses intellectual symbols'.[10] He does not adopt the condescending attitude towards the past that so often characterizes epic philosophies. Nonetheless, the message of his philosophy of technology belongs to the epic manner of describing history. Three propositions of his, in particular, connect him with this perspective and cast him as a philosopher of progress.

The technical mentality

The 'technical mentality'[11] is a driving force of progress. It is a vision of the world that has been transmitted across the ages. Simondon noted its presence among the Ionian physiologists, the alchemists and Descartes, then among the Enlightenment thinkers, and in cybernetics. It constitutes a foundational layer in the history of Western rational thought. Judged prematurely, says Simondon, it risks appearing 'monstrous and mentally unbalanced'. It is analytical. The technical mentality rejects the holistic notion that all living beings constitute intangible totalities which must be respected as they are. This notion is perhaps nothing more than a facile solution to a complex problem. Technologists favour timely, targeted interventions over global judgements. They look for places in the world where localized intervention could increase rationality and overcome natural imperfections.

The technical mentality has always existed. Simondon finds in his exploration of history – the history of computer science, for example – a repetition of common themes: the desire to delegate long calculations, the need to obtain reliable results, and the need for a material means of storing memory. The same goals motivated numerous

---

[10] *Mode d'existence*, p. 91.
[11] Simondon devotes numerous analyses to this concept throughout his oeuvre.

inventors: Pascal built his machine to help his father, a tax commissioner in Normandy, with his calculations, Babbage was concerned with census calculations, and the American government approached Von Neumann during the war, asking him to establish calculation tables for use in aiming ballistics missiles; today, software is being developed to measure the size of the internet.

Cybernetics brings ancient desires to fruition. It also continues the ancient battle against the sacred or ideal signification of numbers. For the Pythagoreans, numbers represented man, woman, perfection and harmony. They were the essence of things. The tetrahedron recapitulated the hidden structure of the universe.[12] The technical mentality functions on a different level. Each of the 'actors' in the history of information science assigned a functional role to numbers. The zeros and ones of binary logic have no intrinsic meaning: they merely occupy a position in space.[13]

The history of computer science appears more epic than contingent from the point of view of a technical mentality. For Simondon, this state of mind was always at work throughout the history of humanity. From the Enlightenment thinkers to cybernetics, it is as if this spirit were pursuing its own '*technophanie*'.[14]

---

[12] Ernst Jünger examined the desacralization of numbers in *Numbers and Gods* (*Zahlen und Götter*), translated into French as *Les Nombres et les Dieux*, trad. F. Poncet, Paris: Bourgois, 1995.

[13] The technical mentality also opposes the interpretation of numbers as 'idealities'. In the twentieth century, Husserl was the most eloquent voice in defence of this idealism. In his *Philosophy of Arithmetic*, he notes that the abacus was a mechanical arrangement capable of supporting 'blind thought'. He contrasts this with the idealized conception in which numbers have a signification that transcends their material form. Husserl draws a dividing line: on one side, signs whose signification is determined exclusively by the practical conventions governing the system; on the other, signs that have intrinsic significations. In Husserl's reckoning, the West lost access to meaning and gained itself a crisis, by neglecting the ideal aspect of significations.

[14] This term appears in the course on the *Psycho-sociologie de la technicité* (*Psycho-sociology of technicity*), *op cit.* Translator's note: a neologism apparently modelled on 'theophany' (*théophanie*) – a visible manifestation of a deity – from the Greek θεοφάνεια (*theophania*), 'appearance of god'. *Technophanie* seems to refer to the manifestation or realization of a technological conceit.

Every object has a nucleus

Simondon distinguishes two 'layers' in an object: an internal layer –
the technical nucleus (*noyau technique*), and an external layer. The
former is the true zone of technological activity. The combustion
chamber of a motor, the engine of an aeroplane, or the micropro-
cessor of a computer respond only to technological pressures. Hidden
from the scrutiny of the uninitiated, they cannot be modified without
affecting their performance. They are technological black boxes. The
nucleus is covered by an external layer, the superficial form which
'materializes' human values and fashions – what Simondon calls
'psycho-social inferences'.[15] The interior design of an ocean liner
or the colour of a car may vary. The external layer, important as it
may be to the user, is non-essential from a technical point of view.
Descartes believed that the object is double. He differentiates between
secondary qualities (flavour, texture, colour) and primary qualities
which are objective, i.e. constitutive of the object: its size, shape
and material composition. Simondon reiterates this distinction. He
separates the essence from the inessential, the technological constant
from social variations. The depth of his analysis is made possible
by this bracketing of the inessential. By focusing exclusively on the
essence of technology, he discovers its guiding principles. The law of
miniaturization, for example, is a principle specific to information
technologies. Miniaturization is neither a response to a challenge
nor a constraint imposed by the way in which technologies are used.
The thermodynamics industry has been pushed towards gigantism
because energetic output increases with size. In contrast, the output
of information channels increases proportionately as the size of the
machine decreases. Finding the 'right' dimension is a technological
problem. In some cases, it took thousands of attempts by thousands

---

[15] Cf. *Psycho-sociologie de la technicité*.

of people to produce the 'perfect' object. The shape of church bells has remained essentially unchanged since the eleventh century AD. The shapes produced by computer modeling 'line up' exactly with the original shapes constructed by master bell makers.[16] Nine centuries of evolving mentalities have had no effect on the technical nucleus.

This distinction between the essence and the inessential links Simondon to the epic presentation of history. It compels him to distinguish between two evolutions: the evolution of the core of the object and that of its external layer. The evolution of the automobile is measured in terms of the power of motors and the effectiveness of the solutions applied to problems of transmission or braking. True progress occurs at the internal level. The layout, design and ergonomics are of comparatively minor importance, their form dictated by fashion or habit.

The contingent presentation of history rejects this distinction. It does not minimize the importance of technology, but it connects technology to the other dimensions. In *Aramis, or the love of technology*, Latour gives an account of the evolution of a project to build a new metro system in Paris.[17] Engineers, politicians, and financiers all have a hand in the venture. Each of them attempts to impose their interests on the plans for the project. Latour demonstrates that this process of concretization resists the distinction between the technological and the psycho-social. A key figure in his book is the old woman carrying parcels. She haunts the dreams of the engineers, because building a metro also means thinking about her movements as she enters the train car and sits down. The quality of the vehicle's brake system reflects concern for this old woman, as much as it does the capabilities of French technology. When the system is considered

---

[16] Cf. on this subject Y. Desforge's postface to Simondon's *Mode d'existence des objets techniques*, pp. 294 and 295.

[17] Cf. B. Latour, *Aramis ou l'amour des techniques*, Paris: La Découverte, 1993.

from a global perspective, it becomes apparent that what is essential is not always confined to the interior of the black box.

Good coupling

Cybernetics invented a new relationship between people and machines. Simondon celebrates this. He demonstrates that information technologies represent a real step forward: they allow for the successful coupling of human and machine. In traditional societies, the connection between humans and machines remained underdeveloped. Rationalized by the Enlightenment thinkers, in practice it remained confined to artisanal guilds. The nineteenth century saw the proliferation of machines, and with it an increase in societal malaise. Finally, the emergence of cybernetics created an opportunity for the establishment of an appropriate relationship between human beings and their technologies.

Simondon demonstrated this using the example of memory. The human memory is sensitive to the content of the remembered experience. It selectively stores those details that interest and emotionally affect it. It forges connections between different, and sometimes temporally distant, situations. It is poorly suited for retaining random strings of numbers or the positions of miscellaneous objects placed on a table. The human memory requires internal structures and filters, which it creates for itself. The machine's memory, in contrast, 'thrives on multiplicity and disorder'.[18] It retains every detail. Photographic film, magnetic tape and compact disks preserve information point by point. But the machine's memory is indifferent to the value or meaning of this data. It is incapable of selectivity. In a good thriller, the characters with the least in common make the most effective pairings. The same is true in this case: the

---

[18] *Mode d'existence*, p. 122.

two types of memory complement one another. Together, they fulfill "a unique function",[19] that of a two-pronged memory capable of effectively processing order and disorder. Simondon sees in cybernetics a way to move beyond the problems posed by previous stages of technological evolution. Information machines no longer replace human beings. They allow for a collaboration, a 'good' coupling which realizes the ideal of a 'technological life'.

The epic of technology moves towards a specific end. Simondon suggests that the technological life consists not of humans directing machines, but of humans learning 'to exist at the same level as them'.[20] We must be *coupled* with multiple machines. Human beings thus become 'agent(s) and translator(s) of information from one machine to another'.[21] We are part guardian, part servant. We *are*, beyond any sense of alienation.

Today, it must be acknowledged that this couple has arrived. The problems which now, perhaps, present themselves are the quality of the matrimonial regime and the education of the resulting offspring.

[19] *Idem*, p. 124.
[20] *Idem*, p. 125.
[21] 'Prospectus' of *Mode d'existence*, in *Gilbert Simondon, Une pensée de l'individuation et de la technique, op. cit.*, pp. 265-7.

Part Two

Individuation

Simondon sought a philosophy that could account for evolution. A philosophy that was supple and mobile, like the process of becoming itself; a philosophy that followed the genesis of things. He had an aversion to principles: fixed, foundational laws. Evolution does not follow a predetermined course; it is a process. Philosophical investigation of the process of becoming requires a certain modesty. It is relatively easy to speak of principles, which are stable and well defined, but describing a process of evolution demands the flexibility of a contortionist.

Processes of evolution defy linguistic labels. Medieval logicians understood this. It was said of Augustus that he found Rome a city of bricks and left it a city of marble. And yet, we say that the city was the same Rome at the beginning and at the end of his reign. This appeal to principle conceals, with the unchanging identity of a name, the transformation of temples, palaces and avenues. Simondon is more interested in this transformative process than in nominal identities. His is a philosophy of genesis. In each order of reality, he challenges notions of identity and substance. He presents a 'doctrine' based on one idea: the individual is not a substance, but the result of a process of individuation.

5

The Brick

Aristotle, Saint Thomas of Aquinas and the scholastics subscribed to the idea of hylomorphism: each being is composed of matter, ὑλο- (*hylo-*) and form, μορφή (*morphē*). Form is the determining principle of matter. The scholastics explained changes of substance with the theory of 'substantial mutations'. The conversion of oxygen and hydrogen into water is an example of a change of substance. After the mutation, matter is unchanged, but its form is altered. Form initially determines the substantive being of oxygen and hydrogen and the properties they exhibit. Once the mutation has occurred, the resulting form specifies the properties of water. Individuation – the process of becoming, whereby any individuated entity comes into being – also originates with form. Indeterminate matter alone cannot give rise to individuation. Form is the determining and specifying principle that transforms matter.

For centuries, this theory explained the nature of the world and the phenomenon of change. Descartes contested it, but the idea of determinate form retained its adherents. In the twentieth century, scientific discoveries made such a theory difficult to defend. In 1924, Pedro Descoqs published his 'Critique of hylomorphism',[1] in which he argued that the scholastic theory was accurate from a metaphysical point of view, even if, in practice, it was invalidated by

[1] P. Descoqs, *Essai critique sur l'hylémorphisme*, Paris: Beauchesne, 1924.

experience. Atomism dealt a death blow to the theory of substantive mutation. It makes little sense to speak of indeterminate matter if matter itself is composed of atoms and molecules – specified, measurable entities. Moreover, atomic theory confirms the presence of unchanging elements within objects of diverse chemical composition: oxygen and hydrogen molecules continue to exist within water. This finding is incompatible with the theory that transformations in the appearance of things correspond to substantive mutations. The recombination of chemicals does not produce a new embodiment, in the sense conceived of by Saint Thomas and his disciples. It produces a new arrangement of molecules, not a genuinely new substance.

Simondon's theory of individuation intercedes in this debate, reversing the tenets of hylomorphism: form is not a determining principle, and matter is not indeterminate. For Simondon, the process of brick making confirms this thesis. What does he observe in this process, where others had perceived the meeting of form and matter?

To make a brick, the brick maker fills a wooden mould with clay. Simondon argues that this clay is not indeterminate matter. Extracted from marshy soil, it is 'dried out, ground into powder, immersed in water, kneaded for a long time': it has already been formed. Its molecular properties determine its quality, porosity and density. As for the mould, it is by no means a pure form. It is made from wood that is relatively robust, but still malleable. The artisan adds a powdered coating to the inner walls of the mould, to ensure that the finished brick will slide out easily. The form is itself matter that has been treated.

On closer examination, the initial conditions of hylomorphism put forth by the scholastics must be reconceived. We must replace the pure concepts of form and matter with the concept of a formed matter and a material form. The firing of the brick takes us even further: the clay compressed in its mould rises in the kiln. The walls of the mould apply an opposing force. Clay and mould interact with one another as forces. At the molecular level, their 'relation' is explained by the release of energy through combustion. According to Simondon, scholastic theory presents this stage of transformation as a 'dark zone (*zone obscure*)'. Hylomorphism speaks of a meeting between form and matter, without explaining the conditions of this encounter. But the dark zone is a relation between forces. 'It is as *forces* that matter and form are brought together'.[2] The relation is not mysterious, it is physical.

'The relation has the value of being (*La relation a valeur d'être*)': this is the motto for a philosophy of individuation. The relation does not connect A and B once they have already been constituted. It is operative from the start. It is interior to their being. The relation is not an accidental feature that emerges after the fact to give the substance a new determination. On the contrary: no substance can exist or acquire determinate properties without relations to other substances and to a specific milieu. To exist is to be connected. This philosophical proposition allows Simondon to establish the scope of his project: to reconcile being (*l'être*) and becoming (*le devenir*). The relation is becoming in action. It drives the process wherein being undergoes change and the individual evolves. The relation is part of being, just as time is coalescent with reality. In the same way, being and becoming are mutually interdependent. One expresses stasis, the other change. Individuation is not the mid-point between these two extremes, like Aristotle's golden mean. It is the meeting of these two dimensions, wherein the existence of each is made possible by the existence of its opposite. The *yin–yang* is a fitting symbol for Simondon's ontological intuition.

There is nothing strange about borrowing a technical example to address a question of natural philosophy: the concept of hylomorphism was itself likely based on the observation of artisans working

---

[2] *L'Individu et sa genèse*, p. 39.

with matter. Sculpture may be seen as the imposition of form from the mind of the artist on to marble. In the design of a temple, the observer can discern the geometry of form and granite. These observations of technical practice seem to confirm hylomorphism: the work of the artisan imposes form upon matter. But by digging deeper into this question, Simondon observes that the origin of hylomorphism is more social than technical. The superiority of form over matter reflects social organization. The masters, in their observation of technicians, have distinguished form from matter. Their orders contain the forms; they decide what things will become. The slaves operate on the level of matter. Like matter, they mutely await the master's orders and give them form. Hylomorphism is a mentality, a way of seeing. It is not borne out by concrete experience.

6

The Crystal

Simondon shares the cyberneticists' ideal of a unified theory of being, based on the concept of information. This concept extends far beyond the philosophy of technology: it is also applicable to physics, biology and psychology.[1] Information may be understood in three different senses: syntactical, semantic and pragmatic. The first sense concerns problems in the transmission of information. Its initial applications are strictly technical. Questions of syntax concern how information is to be coded, the channels of transmission, the physical capacities of information systems, and issues of redundancy and noise. Information may also be approached from a semantic angle. In this case, the primary concern is the meaning of the symbols that constitute a message. An important issue for semantics is identifying the common conventions that must be shared by the transmitter and receiver of a signal so that the meaning of the information transmitted may be mutually understood. Finally, information lends itself

---

[1] W. R. Ashby writes of cybernetics that it is 'heaven-sent'. It is a bridge between simple systems and hyper-complex ones: 'until recently we have had no experience of systems of medium complexity; either they have been like the watch and the pendulum, and we have found their properties few and trivial, or they have been like the dog and the human being, and we have found their properties so rich and remarkable that we have thought them supernatural. Only in the last few years has the general-purpose computer given us a system rich enough to be interesting, yet simple enough to be understandable .... The computer is heaven-sent ... for it enables us to bridge the enormous conceptual gap from the simple and understandable to the complex and interesting' (W. R. Ashby, 'Principles of the Self-organizing System', in *Mechanisms of Intelligence: Ashby's Writings on Cybernetics*, (ed.) Roger Conant, Seaside, CA: Intersystems Publications, 1981, pp. 66–7. Cited by H. Atlan, *Entre le cristal et la fumée*, Paris: Seuil, 1979, p. 40).

to a pragmatic analysis: How does it affect the behaviours of trans-mitter and receiver?[2]

The pragmatic study of information has more than a few things in common with the scholastic investigation of forms. In both cases, the primary concern is to discover the *effect* of form on matter. The theory of information allows us to reformulate this question.[3] It asks: What is the *effect* of information on the milieu that receives it? Dissatisfied with the logical conception of form, Simondon revisited the medieval question of individuation with the notion of information in hand. Some of the scholastics held that all forms were static. Those who believed in a unique, rigid form maintained that its sole function was its determining effect on matter. This function is diametrically opposed to dynamism: its adherents refused to accept that a form could be active on its own, independent of its role in specifying the properties of individual things. Simondon favoured the opposite interpretation. In his theory, form and action are combined in a single notion: information. 'It is necessary to replace the notion of form with that of information', he wrote.[4] Like the cyberneticists, he viewed information as an operation. Its function is not only one of determination; it causes a mutation, it triggers change. Information becomes the factor that sets in motion the process of individuation. This active role was first described by Simondon in the context of crystallization.

---

[2] Research at the Palo Alto Institute, another heir to the legacy of cybernetics, has focused on the human behavioural aspects of information systems. Cf. P. Watzlawick, J. Helmick Beavin and D. D. Jackson, *Une logique de la communication*, Paris: Seuil, 1972.

[3] In the second part of his introduction to *Individuation Psychique et Collective*, Simondon discusses the question of form as addressed by Plato and Aristotle. He subsequently notes: 'It is necessary to bring to bear upon the theory of information a term not related to probability. It might perhaps be possible – and it is the starting point of my thesis – to speak of a quality of information, or of an informational tension' (p. 52). This tension, as we will see, may be carried like a seed or 'germ'. Individuation depends on the relation between 'informational tension in the structural germ and unformed, metastable potential' (p. 54). Simondon replaces the earlier concept of form with a new theory of information.

[4] *L'individu et sa genèse*, p. 211.

Simondon observed the growth of a crystal in its mother-water. He studied the parameters that determine the nature of a crystal: temperature, pressure, shock, chemical composition. He contemplated ancient sources which saw the perfection of the crystal as a link between the organic and the inorganic. He also studied the refraction of light through crystalline structures and the implications of these structures for atomic theory. Finally, he alighted upon the crystal as the paradigm for his theory of individuation.

At the end of the eighteenth century, the Abbé Haüy advanced the hypothesis that crystals were formed periodically from an 'integral molecule'.[5] From then on, the study of crystals had to move beyond the phenomenological plan of the crystal's external form and try instead to understand its internal, molecular organization, concealed beneath the surface structure of the crystal. Prior to this, crystallography was primarily concerned with problems of classification, inventory, and collection of specimens from mines and volcanic regions. This descriptive activity, accompanied by research into the role of crystals in the formation of the earth, was as much a metaphysical examination as it was a matter of physical exploration. In addition to their many applications in medicinal and magical practices, crystals sparked the imagination and spurred reflection. Jean Buridan (1300–58) attributed the presence of crystals on the earth's surface to a process of 'coagulation' originating at the earth's core, where matter was subjected to very low temperatures. The resulting crystals were brought to the surface through orogenesis, a phenomenon in which rocks are pushed above ground by the pressure of forces emanating from the centre of the earth. Once the rocks had undergone the effects of erosion, the crystals were revealed. This idea of 'coagulation' came from Aristotle and was confirmed by the formation of stalactites. Kepler (1571–1630) was also influenced by

[5] F. Balibar, *La Science du cristal,* Paris: Hachette, 1991, p. 29.

Aristotle in formulating the hypothesis that hexagonal snow crystals had a liquid origin. For Kepler, the arrangement of their crystalline facets was the effect of forces whose geometrical action reflected the soul of the earth.[6] These two examples demonstrate that the process of crystal formation could be linked to cosmogonies. Thus, Buffon saw in the 'figuration' of minerals a principle of organization that he identified as a first step towards life (*'ébauche de vie'*),[7] due to the presence of organic molecules. The crystal exists at the border between two realities. Although it belongs to the class of minerals, its organization, its genesis and its beauty prompted many philosophers and scientists to perceive in it the vestiges of a common ancestry with living things. Jean-Claude de la Métherie spoke of the 'crystallisation of the foetus'. He also viewed the soul, which is the centre of being, as the result of a crystallization. The process of crystallization went beyond the domain of mineralogy. Identified with organic processes, crystallization was for a long time viewed as the 'missing link' between organic and inorganic matter. The perfectly ordered structure of the inorganic crystal, and its genetic formation starting with a 'germ' or seed, which the Greeks called *spermata*, led many early scientists to situate crystals at the outermost edge of the inorganic and thus, for those who took a 'continuist' view of evolution, at the frontiers of the organic.[8]

The discoveries made by Romé de l'Isle and Haüy in the eighteenth century put an end to these speculations. Simondon demonstrates, nonetheless, that a thorough understanding of the physics of crystals can lead to speculative conclusions that go far beyond physics. The crystal, paradigm of individualization, constitutes for Simondon an

---

[6] Cf. D. Lecourt, 'Introduction', in F. Balibar, *La science du cristal, op. cit.*, p. 11.

[7] *Idem*, p. 12.

[8] Thus, the botanist Joseph Pitton de Tournefort (1656–1708) wrote: 'The different species of pyrites, rock crystals, and an infinity of other stones can be supposed to originate from seeds (*germes*), like mushrooms, truffles, and many species of moss for which we have yet to discover their method of propagation.'

opportunity to reaffirm the connections between the phases of being and becoming. Moreover, the crystal occupies a strategic position: it serves as the model for physico-chemical individuation, which Simondon will use as the starting point for his theory of biological individuation.[9] Thus, in Simondon's hands, the object of scientific study becomes a subject for philosophical reflection.

Form and matter do not explain the genesis of the crystal. They allow us to formulate a theory *a posteriori*, when the crystal has already been individuated. But if we follow the process of individuation step by step, other observations present themselves. The milieu in which a crystal first forms is its mother-water, a substance (*matière*) which crystallographers describe as 'amorphous', to emphasize that its molecules are in an unstable, disordered state, lacking, above all, the periodic order which determines the geometry of the crystal. The amorphous substance must be in a *meta-stable* state to produce a crystal: it must be at a temperature that will support rapid evolution. Crystallization will not occur if the environment is too stable.

The introduction of a 'germ' into the mother-water initiates the process. The germ is a foreign body or a shock to the system. It is a piece of information – that is, an element (or an event) that is singular and new.[10] The germ introduces an asymmetry into the amorphous

---

[9] Such is the case in the first edition of *L'individu et sa genèse physico-biologique* published by the P.U.F. (Presses Universitaires de France) in 1964. The Millon (1995) edition includes a supplementary section entitled 'Form and Substance' (*Forme et substance*) which consists of 85 pages copied from the thesis submitted to the Sorbonne in 1958 (shelf mark W1958 (33), printed in quarto). This supplementary section is devoted to an interpretation of quantum mechanics. It is inserted between a section devoted to crystals and one devoted to life, but it should be noted that in the final section of the chapter 'Form and Substance', entitled 'Topology, chronology, and order of magnitude of physical individuation' (*Topologie, chronologie et ordre de grandeur de l'individuation physique*), Simondon returns to the problem of the crystal and hypothesizes that 'the individuation of life inserts itself into physical individuation by suspending its course, slowing it down, making it capable of propagation to the inchoate state. The living individual is in some sense, at its most primitive levels, a crystal in its nascent state, growing in its metastable environment', (*L'individu et sa genèse*, p. 150).

[10] The appearance of a germ in the amorphous meta-stable fluid is 'spontaneous, and to date inexplicable', writes Simondon (*L'individu et sa genèse*, p. 102). He rejects the probabilistic explanation. It does not seem possible to give an 'explanation' for this appearance,

substance. 'It has the value of a principle':[11] it provides energy and transmits a structure to the substance that it did not previously possess. It brings geometry to the substance: cube, pyramid, octahedron, rhomboid.... It is the first layer of the crystal. Its structure polarizes the material around it, triggering a corresponding change in structure and release of energy. The newly transformed structure thus serves as the germ for the transformation of matter further from the nucleus. The limits of the crystal expand outward. Its growth is the propagation of order in chaos.

Becoming is not opposed to being. Becoming is 'the relation that constitutes the being as individual'.[12] It is not only that pure movement, that process disconnected from any support, which opposes the stability of being. Simondon looked for compatibility between these two aspects of individuation. He sought to treat them as a mixture, not wanting to confine being to a rigid substantialism in which it would be essentially insusceptible to mutations, nor to compress becoming into an immaterial energeticism. The example of the crystal furnished him with a model for thinking about the coalescence of being and becoming. In what sense can we say that the crystal is a mixture of being and becoming? The individuation of the crystal unfolds between two realities: the already structured crystal and the inchoate milieu, capable of being structured. For Simondon, the already structured crystal symbolizes being, that which is present and given, while the dynamic, energized milieu symbolizes becoming,

---

since the germ might be a speck of dust, or any other physical entity, as long as it has an effect on the meta-stable milieu. This remark by Simondon reveals that the origin of the germ is a blind spot within his doctrine. The germ is envisaged here as a piece of information. In information theory, information may appear at random without *being* random, since its content is distinguishable from pure noise. This classic antinomy of information theory, noted in *Mode d'existence*, p. 136, guides Simondon's description of crystallization to the point of shifting its focus: the problem is not to find out the origin of the germ, but to discover the conditions under which it will be able to have an effect, just as information is distinguished from pure noise, which has no effect, other than to produce static.

[11] *L'individu et sa genèse*, p. 84.
[12] *Idem*, p. 89.

a virtuality that awaits determination. If 'thought' considers only these two states, the crystalline and the crystallizable, it remains in a conflictual situation that presents an impossible choice. If it chooses the crystal and thereby presents itself as a 'thought of being', it misses becoming and cannot explain the modifications, progressions or actualizations of virtualities. Similarly, if this thought chooses the dynamic, energized milieu as its model for becoming, it becomes, as it were, evanescent, a pure contemplation of virtualities. In Simondon's view, by reflecting on the process of crystallization, we can provide a solution to this conflict. The two preceding positions each depend on a particular state of matter. Simondon chooses the milieu and the operation. Between the already formed crystal and the structurable milieu exists the limit of the crystalline individual. 'The limit', explains Simondon, 'is neither potential nor structure'. It is neither the past of the crystal nor its future. It is the point where growth is occurring in the crystalline individual at a given moment in time. Potential and structure, past and future communicate on this shifting frontier. Combining being and becoming, the limit is never completely one or the other. It is the here-and-now (*lieu-moment*) of individuation, the point where that which is and that which is becoming interact. It is this reality that Simondon sought to visualize in order to resolve the antinomy of being and becoming: the here-and-now of what he called 'transduction' – the propagation of information in an amorphous milieu.

This amorphous milieu, rich in energy but lacking structure, is a self-organizing chaos. Simondon was aware of a limitation of language.[13] It is impossible to speak of chaos without reference to some kind of order. The adjective "amorphous", which bears the mark of an absence,[14] defines a milieu in terms of its lack of form. Chaos has

---

[13] 'The concepts are adequate only for individuated reality' (*L'individu et sa genèse*, p. 25).
[14] Translator's note: because it begins with the prefix of negation: *a-*, 'not'.

no logical positivity of its own. It is not individuated. But Simondon plays time against logic. Rather than expressing it in negative terms, he describes chaos as the 'not yet'. The empty glass is not yet full. The chaotic milieu is not yet individuated: it is 'pre-individual'. It is awaiting individuation; the necessary energetic conditions have already been met; all it lacks is a germ to initiate the process. In Aristotelean terms, the pre-individual would be potency without action – a pure passivity. But Simondon rejects this terminology: Aristotle gives primacy to the act and defines potency in terms of that which the act is lacking. This conception of potency is framed in terms of logical absence (i.e. negation). And yet, the pre-individual is positive. It is a generative and creative potency. Its potency is a vitality that is still untamed, a pure nature, a *physis*, a *natura naturans*. The pre-individual is nature seized at its source, nature still untouched by determination, formless and limitless, but already full of a vitality that will be shaped by determination.

Anaximander called this radical origin ἄπειρον (*apeiron*),[15] a concept which Simondon makes his own. The pre-individual is nature in a pre-Socratic sense. It is the reservoir of becoming. The pre-Socratics were, for Simondon, the true thinkers of individuation. Their worldview was not informed by the fascination with the individuated being which dominated later philosophies and forced an understanding of reality as the sum of all individuated things. They did not settle upon a principle of individuation, a first term from which individuals develop, as a monad unfolds its essence. They had the intuition of a verb (*to grow*) and of a milieu as yet unformed, 'phase-less (*sans phase*)', but alive. The 'pre-individual',

---

[15] Marcel Conche explains that for Anaximander, 'the apeiron is neither matter (ὕλο-/ *hylo-*), nor an intermediary (μεταξύ/*metaxu*) between two elements (such as water and fire, water and air, etc.), nor a mixture (μίγμα/*migma*)'. The apeiron is doubly indeterminate: physically, since it has no topological demarcations, and logically, because it precedes categorical determinations. Cf. *Anaximandre. Fragments et témoignages*, (ed.) M. Conche, Paris: P.U.F., 1991, p. 87.

which Simondon postulated to refer to the milieu of individuation prior to the emergence of the individual, is Anaximander's *apeiron*. It is rare for Simondon to borrow a concept. In fact, this particular borrowing is unique in his philosophy. His other borrowings, from Plato or Descartes, always concern processes, operations, ways of doing or organizing, but never, as here, the name of a phase of being.[16] Simondon's privileged relationship with the pre-Socratics explains this borrowing. They were thinkers and technicians. 'For them', wrote Simondon, 'the present reality of the world is understood by its genesis, and cosmogony is tangible and concrete like the progressive change of state undergone by clay as it absorbs more water under the hand of the potter'.[17] Their thought also belonged to a time of beginnings; they preceded the history of philosophy, which Simondon views as the history of the rediscovery of individuation by the already constituted individual. The pre-Socratic influence is apparent at yet another level. In the same way that Anaximander imagines the *apeiron* to be determined by a *gonimon* (γόνιμον: 'that which is capable of engendering'), Simondon explains that the pre-individual is determined by information.

[16] The pre-individual is the first phase of being.
[17] Course on *Perception, op. cit.*, p. 570. In his book *Early Greek Science*, the British historian G. E. R. Lloyd noted that even if the sources of information about Ionian technology in the fourth century AD are exceedingly limited, it has been established that this technology provided the basis for the naturalist explications of the physiologists. Cf. Lloyd, *Early Greek Science: Thales to Aristotle*, New York: W. W. Norton & Co, 1970. According to the German philologist Bruno Snell, it was Empedocles whose analogies were the least anthropomorphic and most concerned with inanimate nature. Nevertheless, 'Anaximander and Anaximenes were also familiar with technical analogies, but since we have only incomplete remnants of their theories, we know less about the details, much less their formulation, than we do with Empedocles'. Cf. B. Snell, *La découverte de l'esprit: la genèse de la pensée européenne chez les Grecs* (trans. M. Charrière and P. Escaig), Combas: L'éclat, 1994, p. 287. It should be noted, by way of qualification, that Conche rejects the strictly empiricist interpretation, recalling the role of thought in the selection of natural analogies: 'The processes by which things have become that which they are must be discovered in, and according to, the result being examined – namely, the world – and that can only be achieved through Thought' in *Anaximandre*, (ed.) M. Conche, *op. cit.*, p. 79. But this thought is nourished by an empirical study of transformations.

7

Coral Colonies

The scholastics recognized that when a man eats, he incorporates the substance of the food. He makes its form and its matter his own. It is necessary, then, to acknowledge that this man is determined by two forms: his own and that of his food. Saint Thomas considered this a perilous consequence. The unity of man is ruptured if another form exists within him. He is no longer substantially one, but two, or several. This is tantamount to saying that man is determined by a principle other than the soul, which is contradictory, since the soul is the one defining principle of individuation.

The scholastics got around this difficulty by means of the theory of substantial mutation. Ingested foods lose their form. They are corrupted, degenerating back into unformed matter before submitting to a new determination, that of the soul that presides in this body. Pedro Descoqs, in the essay cited earlier, shows that this solution is artificial. Ingested foods retain some of their essential properties. Salts remain salts; minerals preserve their chemical structure. Conversely, the body's cells each have a form and can subsist outside the body in tissue cultures. Descoqs therefore advocates for a pluriformist conception, already championed by medieval scholars: the body contains millions of determining principles. This does not prevent us from affirming that, from a metaphysical perspective, man is still determined by a single substantial principle.

This debate is of the utmost importance for the philosophy of individuation. What is an individual? A single, indivisible being. But when human beings eat food, do they become double? One could say of the individual what Saint Augustine said of time: everyone knows what it is, but no one can explain it. Etymology is of no help. The individual is 'indivisible', yet life is maintained within the individual through a process of cellular division. This peculiarity of language is a symptom of the problem. It is also occurs in atomism: the 'a-tom' is, by definition, indivisible, yet what energy is spent on splitting it into subatomic particles![1]

Simondon brought a new method to bear on this debate. He examined the processes involved rather than starting from first principles. Metaphysical necessities were of little concern to him. He rejected the idea that matter is animate because it possesses a principle of animation. As a philosopher of science, he saw in the passage from inert matter to living entity the emergence of new processes. The difference between a crystal and a macro-molecule in organic chemistry is a difference of information. When a crystal is first formed, a single piece of information initiates the process of individuation: the germ unfurls its structure, giving form to matter. The molecule, however, can receive multiple pieces of information. It may be modified by one chemical reaction, then another. It can itself become a source of information for a bacterium. It changes constantly. It integrates and differentiates between pieces of information.

The living entity (*le vivant*) is characterized by a plurality of inputs and outputs, unlike the crystal which is the result of a single initial input.[2] Living things possess multiple 'systems of information

---

[1] Translator's note: The words 'individual' and 'atom' both literally mean 'indivisible': 'individual' from the Latin *individuus*; *in-* 'not' + *dividere* 'to divide', and 'atom' from the Greek ἄτομος (*atomos*); ἀ- (*a-*) 'not' + τέμνω (*temnō*) 'I cut'.

[2] In his book *What is Life* (1943) Erwin Schrödinger establishes a parallel between chromosomes and crystals. The chromosome contains, encoded in a miniature code script, 'the entire pattern of the individuaƖ›s future development and of its functioning in the mature state'. In this respect, the chromosome is no different from the crystal, since the latter also develops from a limited number of repeating configurations. François Jacob writes regarding this idea of Schrödinger's: 'For reasons of stability, the organisation of life becomes similar to that of a crystal. Not the somewhat dull and

(*régimes d'information*). Furthermore, their reactions to information received are at times deferred or indirect. Information must be processed. The living entity digests information and determines the appropriate response. It is a network. Contrary to the theories of the scholastics, multiplicity is not a property of forms, but a feature of systems that regulate activity: nutrition, chemical defence mechanisms, etc. These systems of activity presuppose the existence of an internal milieu that is specific to life.

The Great Barrier Reef in Australia is 2400 km (roughly 1500 miles) long. It is sometimes considered the largest life form on earth. But is it an individual? According to Simondon, a colony of micro-organisms is not a unique being. This criterion for individuation is based on appearances: it is topological. The spatial proximity of micro-organisms does not, on its own, imply the existence of a unique being. Simondon prefers to focus on the roles of different elements within the colony. He notes that certain 'sub-individuals' specialize in nutrition, while others serve a sexual function, or specialize in defence. Each subdivision has its role. There is no centralized coordination. Moreover, the birth and death of these 'sub-individuals' is for each one singular and independent of the rest of the colony. Simondon sees in this a criterion for defining individuality: the individual reproduces and dies. A colony is therefore not an individual. In a study of Simondon's biology, Anne Fagot-Largeault

---

monotonous crystalline structure where a single chemical configuration repeats itself over and over, with the same periodic intervals in three dimensions. But what physicists call an "aperiodic crystal", in which the arrangement of non-repeating configurations creates the variety necessary to support the diversity of living beings. A small number of compositional elements is sufficient for this, adds Schrödinger. With Morse code, the combination of just two symbols allows us to represent any text. With a combination of chemical symbols, it is possible to map out the blueprint of an entire organism. Heredity functions like a calculator's memory' (F. Jacob, *La logique du vivant* (*The Logic of Life*), *op. cit.*, p. 274). The terms of comparison are identical for Schrödinger and Simondon, but they make use of these terms for entirely different purposes. Simondon does not use the crystal to demonstrate that the chromosome activates a code, but to show that the living entity integrates and differentiates between singularities. In Simondon's work, the crystal does not serve an analytical biology but a biology of the 'life-agent (*vivant-agent*)'.

characterizes this classic position: 'The individual in a strict biological sense is, thus, the organism.'[3]

'This is not a doctrine of materialism.'[4] It assumes that there is a connection between physical reality and biological reality, but that the two are not identical in nature. Materialism expects that the two will be identical. Simondon's philosophy, on the other hand, examines the continuities and discontinuities along the chain of connections between the physical and the real. One example of continuity is that of the relation between the meta-stability of systems and the capacity to receive information. A corresponding discontinuity exists between the direct systems of information at the physico-chemical level and the relayed systems of information that are characteristic of life. Discontinuity, which corresponds to the crossing of a threshold, cannot be used to establish distinctions between genus and species. Simondon points to another way of establishing different classifications of reality. These classifications are based on the types of information processes that the system is subject to in the course of its individuation. Information processes may include active properties, systems, or the organizing processes that act upon matter (polarities).

Simondon rejects the initial postulate of materialism, according to which inert nature does not conceal within itself a higher organization. With this postulate, materialism seeks to reduce living systems to simple systems, which are by all indications purely 'material'. But this postulate leads to the idea that the physical world consists entirely of matter, that it *is* substance. This presents an impoverished notion of matter, depriving it of all that could account for physical individuation: potential energies and relations. 'Materialism does not take information into account.'[5] More precisely, it *only* takes information

---

[3]   A. Fagot-Largeault, 'Individuation in biology', in *Gilbert Simondon. Une pensée de l'individuation et de la technique, op. cit.,* pp. 19–54, p. 22.
[4]   *L'individu et sa genèse,* p. 156.
[5]   *Idem.*

into account when considering the later stages in the evolution of species. Materialism valorizes these more 'advanced' stages, while devaluing the organization of inert matter. This approach, says Simondon, reveals a doctrine of values and even an 'implicit spiritualism: matter is taken to be less richly organized than living beings, and materialism seeks to demonstrate that the superior can emerge from the inferior'.[6] For Simondon, who is fully aware that he is going against tradition, and that his hypotheses may appear 'quite surprising', the physical world is already highly organized. Certain large metastable molecules in organic chemistry reveal organizations as complex as those found in the most elementary forms of life. But life is not a substance distinct from matter. Only physical structures can support the processes of integration and differentiation.[7]

The pages concerning the biology of the ocean floor introduce a theoretical invention which reappears elsewhere in Simondon's analyses. After describing the typical organization of coral colonies, he considers the behaviour of what he calls the 'pure individual'. This pure individual detaches itself from its colony of origin, allows itself to be carried by the ocean currents and, far away, deposits eggs that will give rise to a new colony. The pure individual is a pioneer. It abandons the habitual functions of nutrition, defence and reproduction within the colony. Its existence is a bridge. 'It does not belong to a colony,' says Simondon, 'it inserts itself between two colonies without being integrated into either, and its beginning and end are in equilibrium, in that it comes from one community but engenders another; it is (a) *relation*'.[8] The pure individual is also the human being who disregards

---

[6] *Idem.*
[7] Simondon frequently returns to the metaphor of the crystal to address questions of psychology and philosophy. For a critical analysis of the role of the crystal in his thought, cf. I. Stengers 'Comment hériter de Simondon?', in *Gilbert Simondon. Une pensée opérative*, (ed.), J. Roux Publications de l'Université de St. Étienne, 2002, pp. 300–23. See also P. Chabot, *L'éncyclopédie idéale de Simondon* in the same volume.
[8] *L'individu et sa genèse*, p. 167.

social conventions, to be guided only by basic generative and thana-tological instincts. This pure individual is faithful to the fundamental aspects of individuation. Unaffected by the habits of the community, the pure individual propagates and exalts individuation, instead of allowing it to be obscured by routine. Such is the case of the inventor who pursues the new and novel, disregarding communal resistance to change.[9]

Individuation must be understood in two ways. It is, first of all, synonymous with evolution. It explains individual development, life and death. In this sense it is universal. But the analogy between the wandering micro-organism and the socially emancipated human being already discloses a particular vision of the world. Individuation is a general framework. It allows for infinite arrangements. It diver-sifies as living entities become more complex. In another sense it supposes choices, value judgements, fatalities. It remains universal: the fundamentals are fixed. But it is also singular. Individuation is a way of telling the story of life. It is a projective test, in which everyone sees what they want to see. These singular qualities become more evident when Simondon addresses issues of psychology and sociology.

---

[9] Whitehead makes use of the analogy between animal colonies and human beings for other purposes. He shows that 'understanding' and 'routine' are to be found in both contexts. 'Now it is the beginning of wisdom', he writes, 'to understand that social life is founded upon routine. Unless society is permeated, through and through, with routine, civilization vanishes .... The two extremes of complete understanding and of complete routine are never realized in human society. But of the two, routine is more fundamental than understanding, that is to say, routine modified by minor flashes of short-range intelligence.' His analysis, less radical than Simondon's, accords a central place to those small variations which do not appear to be inventions, so deeply are they ingrained in the habits of a society, but which nonetheless, by virtue of the moment at which they appear, the slight variations they introduce, or their style, can advance the progress of understanding. Whitehead's pragmatism makes him dubious of the 'pure individual' or 'complete understanding' as concepts. 'Indeed,' he says, 'the notion of complete understanding controlling action is an ideal in the clouds, grotesquely at variance with practical life.' A.N. Whitehead, *Adventures of Ideas*, New York: The Macmillan Company, 1933, pp. 114–15.

8

Psyche and Society

Human beings experience many types of individuation. Human development is not, after all, exclusively biological. Consequently, human beings cannot overcome their problems through purely physical means. Tensions remain. The psyche emerges in an attempt to resolve these tensions in a new way: with thought. Psychic individuation refers to the evolution of the mental universe in an individual. It is a relationship with the world based on perception, emotion and signification. Being human, for the Thomists, meant having a soul. Simondon rejects this essentialism: he sees the tell-tale sign of humanity in the psychic capacities that constitute a thinking being within the body of a living being.

Psychic evolution goes beyond the individual: it leads the individual towards others. The genesis of sensations and affects already bears witness to this. Human beings orient themselves to the world by sensing relative heat or cold, softness or roughness. Sensations enable them to form a summary image of their environment. Perception complicates this sensual relationship with the world. It localizes the source of warmth in a stone heated by the sun. It understands the cause of a tingling sensation when it sees the object that has been touched. It is through perception that human beings engage with the world: we attach a mental signification to material sensations.

Affect gives rise to a second orientation: that of the human being in relation to himself. Pleasure, approval, discomfort or pain: affects are fleeting and unconscious. They are the signals that indicate the state of our inner world. Emotion takes hold of this primitive material and gives it meaning. It brings together an affect of discomfort, another of pain in the foot and a third of frustration; it stabilizes them, interprets them, and gives them a consistency that can be formulated: an emotion of anger. Emotion persists. It is conscious. It frees the individual from the proximity to himself that mute affect imposes upon him, allowing him to explore the signification of his feelings.

This theory is diametrically opposed to Sartre's theory of emotions. In his *Sketch for a Theory of the Emotions* (*Esquisse d'une théorie des émotions*, 1939), Sartre explains that emotions arise when action is blocked:

> When the paths traced out become too difficult, or when we see no path, we can no longer live in so urgent and difficult a world. All the ways are barred. However, we must act. So we try to change the world, that is, to live as if the connection between things and their potentialities were not ruled by deterministic processes, but by magic.[1]

Emotion, for Sartre, is the direct consequence of a blockage, an insoluble problem. Cornered by a ferocious beast in a back alley, the Sartrean individual can do nothing. The situation is blocked, the paths usually taken are impassable. The conscious mind is overcome with emotion. The individual blacks out. Sartre based this theory on the experimental findings of Tamara Dembo, a German psychologist of the 1930s who conducted laboratory experiments on the nature of anger.[2] She told her experimental subjects that she wanted to measure their competence and skill in resolving problems. The subjects each received a set of plastic rings, which they had to toss on to the neck

---

[1] J. P. Sartre, *Esquisse d'une théorie des émotions*, Paris: Hermann, 1939. Originally published in English as *Emotions: Outline of a Theory*, trans. B. Frechtman, New York, 1948.

[2] Cf. V. Despret, *Ces émotions qui nous fabriquent*, 'Les Empêcheurs de penser en rond', Paris: Synthélabo, 1999, p. 129.

of a bottle. They tried and got nowhere: the bottle was too far away, the rings were too narrow. Dembo also asked her subjects to touch a flower positioned in one corner of the room without crossing a line drawn on the floor around them, which separated them from the flower by several metres. However much they twisted and turned, it was to no avail: the flower remained out of reach. Anger ensued. The experiment was designed to present the subjects with situations in which they could not succeed. The subjects believed that they were being tested on their competence and skill. They were frustrated. Dembo did not hesitate to taunt and mock them for their incapacity.

When an experiment of this kind is used to investigate human thought, the resulting theory must be considered highly particular and restricted in its significance. In claiming that emotion is produced when action is blocked, in characterizing emotion as an escape, or an irrational response, Sartre is merely applying the localized findings of Dembo's experiment to a generalized context. In this experiment, the subjects feel isolated and inferior – and with reason, since they are being mocked and have no means of escape from the trap into which they have been lured, other than feelings of anger and humiliation. Who would not be angry? But to pass from this localized experiment to a general theory of the emotions requires a considerable leap.[3]

Simondon approaches individuation as a problem-solving strategy. Perception brings a solution to the problem posed by a flood of sensations of unknown origin. Emotion brings order to the chaos of our affects. Yet these solutions generate new problems. The individual evolves in order to resolve tensions, assembling perceptions and emotions in ways that are more stable, more coherent. She learns to be the master of her own psyche. Yet, her perceptions and emotions present her with a new challenge: they are often incompatible.

---

[3] Regarding Sartre's theory, Simondon speaks of a 'reductive supposition, bordering on disingenuousness, that wants to restore emotion to the individual'; cf. *Individuation psychique et collective*, p. 212.

Perceptions supply the individual with perspectives on his environment. His emotions prompt him to adopt different attitudes. These perspectives and these attitudes don't always go together: they may contradict one another. Simondon provides no examples to illustrate this problem, which may not be universal. Do we witness a distressing sight and experience a contrary, happy emotion? Or have a perception of sun accompanied by a sentiment of night? For Simondon there is a problem, and it is the collective that can resolve it. The connection with others stabilizes the individual divided between what he sees and what he feels. He pursues his individuation by integrating with a stable network of shared significations. Psychic individuation is also a social process.

In *L'individuation psychique et collective* (*Psychic and Collective Individuation*), Simondon describes two types of relationships with others. The first is classic: that of the individual as *zoon politikon*. This individual sacrifices to the social game, meeting the 'inter-individual' – the other who occupies a particular place in society and conforms to it. The masks remain in place. Simondon describes a society that is well organized, but lacking in authenticity. Then comes the *trans-individual*: the authentic relation, product of a new individuation. The individual digs deep inside herself, into her affective and emotive resources, and is thus able to connect with the other *as* other. Here, honesty rules. Social or professional status, wealth or poverty can no longer act as blockades against fraternity, friendship and love. The trans-individual gives rise to sincerity. One says what one thinks, does what one says and becomes what one is. Simondon sees examples of this in heroism, saintliness and wisdom. He also invokes Nietzsche's Zarathustra, who retrieves the body of the dead tightrope walker, fallen from his rope and abandoned by the crowd.

The trans-individual experience can also be pursued in solitude. As such, it has an element of mysticism. Simondon evokes Saint Francis of Assisi, whose charity knew no limits. He speaks of a communication 'with superior things'[4] which extends from and goes beyond the individual. This communication is the peak of the individual's evolution. Simondon prefers to keep it free of dogma. He is also distrustful of 'interioristic deviations'. The religion of which he speaks is close to the intuitions of Meister Eckhart:

> Negative theology is perhaps alone in having attempted to conceive of the transindividual as something other than a superior individuality, more extensive, but still as individual as that of the human being; the anthropomorphism that is most difficult to avoid is that of individuality.[5]

[4] *Individuation psychique et collective*, p. 157.
[5] *Idem*, p. 161.

9

Imagination

Simondon devoted a course at the Sorbonne to imagination. His theory broke with modern conceptions of the image. The image is not subjective but intermediate between object and subject. His conception is closer to those of the Ancients: Homer accorded to dreams a force of premonition that was independent of the dreamer; Lucretius saw the image as a simulacrum caused by vapours and possessed of an independent reality. Simondon also assigns an ontological status to images. He shows that imagination leads to invention. It can be materialized to become an object, a situation or an event.

Simondon's course, taught from 1965 to 1966, followed the genesis of the image in all orders of reality to show how it brings together heterogeneous contents, how it extracts from these contents orientations, and how these orientations can be materially realized through invention. Simondon brought together as much evidence as possible to support his hypothesis of an image whose dynamism is at once generative and cyclical. The schema that leads from imagination to invention is relatively simple. But the conceptual developments addressed by the course fade into the background as Simondon conjures up a veritable compendium of biological facts, observations on the politics of the 1960s, mythological reminiscences, dialogues with psychoanalysis, cinematographic images, desires, theories of physics, spirituality and analogies with the animal world. We encounter Shirley Temple (affectionately referred to as the 'optimum baby'), cargo cult practitioners and characters from fairy-tales. There are also experiments on bees, suggestions for making night workers' clothing visible in the dark, a theory of subliminal perception, an explanation of the behaviour of mental calculators, and long passages on toys and games. The whole thing resembles Ferdinand Cheval's Ideal Palace, a whimsical structure of which Simondon was very fond.

Imagination follows a cycle. Before experiencing a situation, the individual anticipates it. She creates an a priori image consisting of projections and desires. Then comes the experience. The confrontation with reality does not overwrite the image. On the contrary, the image remains practically operative. It is a 'pattern' that allows us to distinguish between the predictable and the new. Perception is drawn to the singular, the specific and the unfamiliar. It perceives change and movement. It is able to distinguish them as novel because the images to which it compares them contain the 'normal' elements of a situation. This is how a shepherd knows that he has lost a sheep without having to count the flock. His image of the flock serves as a reference.

The cycle of the image continues after the experience. In memory, it is refined and simplified. It becomes charged with affect. It becomes a symbol. But this symbol remains energetically charged; it is *meta-stable*, that is to say, capable of evolving. It is alive with the contradictions and differences between all of the situations it symbolizes. How are the different images connected? Realism argues that there is a continuity between perception and abstract images, a connection between particular sensations and the images that emanate from them. Idealists like Berkeley and Descartes support a theory of discontinuity. Berkeley argued that images are not drawn from an external reality; Descartes, for his part, was committed to the concept of innate ideas, uninformed by perception. Simondon's theory, on the other hand, is firmly grounded in empiricism. The genesis of the image is rooted in the corporeality of the individual; it develops from perceptions which resound in the individual's subconscious. It is clear that Simondon accepts an empirical basis for the imagination, but he corrects the inductivism of this conception on one point. The summation model supposes that all the images of a single reality are added together to form a generic image. Each of the linden trees seen in nature or on television progressively form an image of a linden tree. But if empiricist induction is right to postulate a connection between experienced realities and the development of images, it errs in homogenizing the different realities encountered. Empiricism does not give priority to any particular experience. It puts them all on the same footing, refusing to acknowledge singularities. It obscures the importance of key moments and defining experiences in the generative development of images.

According to Simondon, priority must be given to the vivid experience that initiates the constitution of a class of images. This experience is the germ of the genesis. It may be an image stumbled upon in a book, or the lasting memory of a chance encounter. It remains a grounding presence – like a tree trunk. Simondon uses this metaphor to explain the constitution of a class of images. The tree trunk does not consist of the sum of all images concerning a reality. Instead, new images insert themselves into this trunk in the direction dictated by the polarity of the initial singularity. When they are in agreement with the germinal image, the new images conserve its direction. However, if they diverge from the initial image, they may graft themselves on as asymmetric outgrowths, to form the branches of this imaginary tree. Taking up Taine's example of the constitution of the image of the araucaria tree,[1] Simondon explains:

---

[1] Translator's note: Cf. Taine, Hyppolite, *On intelligence*, trans. T. D. Haye, London, 1871, pp. 397–8.

There is a first araucaria, an original image of this shrub with its
regular form and thick green stems, which will remain the truest, most
authentic, most prominent in memory, and which will be the source
of the norm for all subsequent impressions. If the first araucaria was
small, with bright green leaves, and planted in dark loam, a bigger,
yellower one will be seen as 'a big, yellow araucaria', and a third as an
araucaria with a smooth trunk or straight branches.[2]

The first impression plays the archetypal role of a model for all
that follows. It is the principle of constitution for a class of images.
The particular interest of this conception lies in the asymmetric
outgrowths that form the branches of the tree. They present an
answer to the canonical problem of induction: the case of white
and black swans. The first swan from which we derived our initial
impression forms the germ for the trunk of our imaginary tree, which
expands with each subsequent sighting of a swan. The Australian
black swan appears marginal, aberrant in relation to its constitutive
class. It branches off from it in an asymmetric fashion, but it does
not reform the original constitution of the class. The class remains
as it was, and the comprehension (in the logical sense) of this class
remains unchanged, even as it extends to include this new case. The
singularity of the black swan does not prevent us from including
the characteristic of whiteness in our comprehension of the class
of swans. Logically, according to the principles of induction, this
characteristic should have disappeared. If it remains, says Simondon,
it is because the network of images does not obey this law. It allows
contradictions to coexist and takes into account the marginality of
the black swan. 'The most important epistemological characteristic of
the memory-image is the independence of extension from comprehension; an understanding based on images is thus different from an
understanding based on classic induction.'[3]

---

[2]   Course on *Imagination and Invention*, op. cit., p.1087.
[3]   *Idem*, p. 1088.

For the logician, the image of this tree presents a contradiction. For Simondon, however, it is the sign of a tension, the mark of the development of an inventive potential. The incompatibility of the different outgrowths leads towards the formation of a symbol. The symbol is a condensation of contradictory experiences. It connects antagonisms and welcomes divergences, forming an energized unity which, once saturated, becomes meta-stable and leads the individual to modify the structure of its organization. Imagination drives invention. An individual who carries the image of a possible reality cannot remain inactive; she compares this image to the reality she sees and tries to weld them together. She invents. The symbol is tested and refined by reality. The inventor overcomes the contradictions of the imaginary by making real the image he has in his head. The examples Simondon gives are technologies (bridges, locomotives) and techno-aesthetic accomplishments (Corbusier's architecture, Xenakis' music). Individuation turns the human being into a builder of worlds.

Part Three

The Bridges

Simondon's oeuvre stands on two pillars, and the bridge that links them has not yet been constructed. Technical concretization and individuation appear to be self-contained concepts. And yet objects are created by individuals whose lives are, in turn, structured around technology. Let us leave aside the question of whether Simondon might have wished to make explicit the nature of this connection had he produced a third volume of writings. Perhaps, for Simondon, the relations between individuals and technologies were already clear. This is not the case for all of us, however. Simondon's work demonstrated that technologies follow a particular logic. It also indicated that individuation culminates in the individual's relationship with the other, with the sacred, and with the imagination. The silence that follows these two lessons is dense with questions. Technologies have transformed society. They are the artillery of a new imagination that has acquired the means to make its desires concrete. Concretization and individuation have begun to converge.

This convergence is a source of fears, fantasies and desires. Ours is a time of transition: at no other point in history has humanity been so close to a physical and psychological transformation. The questions that arise are numerous: which individuations should we develop, which technologies should we favour, which seeming concretizations are mere illusions?

Simondon's philosophy helps to clarify these problems. His vision of the world is informed by his knowledge of technology. In this final part, we will examine the connections between individuation and concretization. They are not always obvious: it is up to the interpreter to bring them to light. They stem from sources that influenced Simondon, from his understanding of the sacred, and from the underlying 'esoteric' knowledge that informs his work. We can recognize them in his attempt to construct a philosophy guided entirely by operations. They give shape to his quest for purity and, ulimately, the ambiguity of his faith in progress.

10

Simondon and Depth Psychology

Individuation according to Jung

What does the idea of individuation contribute to philosophy? The affirmation that beings become individuals seems self-evident. Yet, Simondon presents individuation as a novel concept that marks a rupture with tradition. There must be a hidden meaning.

In Jung's analytic psychology, individuation is seen as a path of ascension, the peak of which is not reached by all who climb it. He first uses the term around 1916, by which time he had already distanced himself from Freud. A text of his from this period is entitled 'Adaptation, individuation, and collectivity'.[1] In this essay, he explains that life necessitates adaptation to external conditions – including the natural environment, but also cultural and social environments – and to internal conditions, such as perceptions that originate from the subject, sometimes without the subject's conscious awareness. Individuals may favour one or the other of these adaptations, depending on their temperaments. According to Jung, neurosis is a disruption of the capacity for adaptation: the individual either focuses excessively on his interior environment, or neglects it entirely in his efforts to adapt to the external environment. Jung's psychology,

---

[1] C. G. Jung, 'Adaptation, individuation, collectivity', in *Collected Works of C.G. Jung*, trans. R. F. C. Hull, Vol. 18, Princeton, NJ: Princeton University Press, 1976, pp. 449–54.

still very close to Freud's in this respect, attempts to re-establish balance with reference to the role of the libido.

The novelty introduced by Jung is the observation that, for some people, adaptation is insufficient. Jung locates the 'practical end' of an analytic relationship at the point where a successful adaptation has been achieved, from a medical and analytical standpoint. But in certain cases, which are 'not so uncommon',[2] the transfer is of an extraordinary intensity. Jung interprets this as an urge that runs counter to adaptation and collectivity. The analysand pretends to adapt perfectly. In reality, she is looking for something else: Jung speaks of an 'urge toward individuation'.

Individuation is at first experienced as a sense of wrongdoing. The subject refuses to adapt to others and their norms. He is not satisfied with the group cohesiveness which society upholds as the ideal. The alternative is 'stepping over into solitude, into the cloister of the inner self'. The subject chooses a route that is off the beaten path; since society is hostile to him, he must pursue 'expiation'. Individuation and collectivity are two divergent orientations. The subject can only atone for his desertion by returning to society after his withdrawal from it, bringing back with him new, positive values. This tribute restores balance, and the human relationship is re-established. This is the experience of love.

Individuation is the central concept of Jung's psychology.[3] It is presented as the harmonizing force that unites two incomplete halves of the psyche. Consciousness should defend its reason and coherence; the chaotic life of the unconscious should follow its own path, to the limits of endurance. And the individual, by combining these two antagonistic poles, should become an indestructible unity: an undivided 'in-dividual', the product of an encounter between two

[2] *Ibid.*, p. 450.
[3] C.G. Jung; A. Jaffé, *Memories, Dreams, Reflections*, trans. Richard and Clara Winston, New York: Random House, 1965, p. 255.

forces, which Jung compares to the hammer and the anvil. The 'iron forged between the two'[4] symbolizes the result of the process.

During the 1930s, Jung became interested in works written by medieval alchemists. 'Good Lord, what nonsense!' he exclaimed at first: 'This stuff is impossible to understand.'[5] But, after repeated attempts, he began to see the expression of a harmonization of opposing principles. The coitus of the King and Queen symbolized the conjunction of opposites. The fruit of their union is the 'self'. The essence of individuation is no longer situated in the rejection of adaptation. 'Differentiation' is only a first step, in which the individual is obliged to discard all inessential identifications, as in a Nigredo.[6] It is followed by a rebirth: the becoming of the self (*Selbstwerdung*). The individual discovers in himself a centre, which is not the centre of his conscious personality, since this is not an egocentric quest. The self also embraces the unconscious psyche. The search for the centre, which is a quest for order and totality, has a cosmic element. The self is not the centre of the individual. It is the 'goal'[7] of an individual who seeks to centre herself in a meaningful universe.

In his autobiography, Jung explains that, at a very young age, he had the feeling of being double. He designates as 'number 1' his conscious, social personality, which conformed to familial conventions and scholastic obligations. This personality lived in the 'here and now'. The 'number 2' personality inhabited another world. He had

---

[4] C. G. Jung, *The Essential Jung*, (ed.) A. Storr, Princeton, NJ: Princeton University Press, 1983, p. 225.

[5] C. G. Jung; A. Jaffé, *Memories, Dreams, Reflections*, New York, Random House, 1965, (trans. Richard and Clara Winston), p. 250.

[6] Translator's note: The Nigredo (*l'Oeuvre au Noir* in French) refers to the first stage in the alchemical magnum opus, the process of creating the philosopher's stone, which would turn base metals to gold. In the Nigredo, all ingredients were to be cleansed and cooked at length to produce a uniform black matter.

[7] 'The self is our life's goal, for it is the completest expression of that fateful combination we call an individual', in The Collected Works of C.G. Jung. 2nd edn, trans. R. F. C. Hull, Vol. 7, Princeton, NJ: Princeton University Press, 1966, p. 404.

the feeling that something other than myself was involved. It was as though a breath of the great world of stars and endless space had touched me, or as if a spirit had invisibly entered the room.[8]

This part of himself, still cloaked in shadow, attracted Jung to Schopenhauer, Kant and the study of theology. 'Where *It* was, *I* must be', declared Freud[9]. In contrast, the motto of Jungian psychology could be: 'Where two are, one individual must be.'

Simondon's Nigredo

The last lines of Simondon's introduction to his *Individuation psychique et collective (Psychic and collective individuation)* make reference to Jung and to alchemy. Simondon writes that he wants to 'generalize the schema'[10] of alchemy.

> The Magnum Opus was begun by dissolving everything in mercury or reducing everything to a carbonized state – until nothing more could be distinguished; the substances lost their limits and their individuality, their isolation; after this crisis and this sacrifice came a new differentiation; it was the Albefactio, then Cauda Pavonis,[11] that brought forth objects from this indistinct blackness, like the light of dawn which distinguishes them by their color. Jung discovered, in the aspirations of the Alchemists, a translation of the operation of individuation, and of all the forms of sacrifice, which supposed a return to a state comparable to that of birth, that is, a return to a state that was rich with potential, but not yet determined, a domain for the renewed propagation of Life.[12]

---

[8] C. G. Jung; A. Jaffé, *Memories, Dreams, Reflections*, New York, Random House, 1965, (trans. Richard and Clara Winston), p. 88.

[9] Translator's note: In the original German, '*Wo Es war, soll Ich werden*'.

[10] *Individuation psychique et collective*, p. 65.

[11] Translator's note: Cauda Pavonis or 'peacock's tail' refers to the stage in the magnum opus that immediately precedes the creation of the philosopher's stone, in which the contents of the alchemist's vessel rapidly change colour.

[12] *Idem.*

Simondon's approach is more comprehensible if we accept this alchemical schema. He began by dissolving everything: being, substances, general ideas, notions of form and matter. He discarded the classical concepts of philosophy to forge a new image of the individual. A large part of his work was negative. He dissolved and incinerated. He practiced a 'Nigredo' on philosophy and on an object of philosophy: the individual. Often, it is true, philosophers begin by positioning themselves in opposition to something. They explain the principles they are rejecting in order to formulate their own ideas. Plato's challenge of Parmenides, his philosophical father, has remained the symbol of this quest for autonomy. Nevertheless, Simondon's departure is more radical. He does not merely split with philosophical tradition. His approach to humanity begins with a *tabula rasa*. He promises that something will emerge from it: the peacock's tail, 'Cauda Pavonis'.

Simondon's book on psychology is striking for its extreme minimalism. He rejects myths, ideas, absolutes, substances and archetypes. He turns away from language, games and shifts in meaning. He empties notions of their content in order to examine their function. He takes a negative approach to mythologies: 'We cannot take account of myth', he declared, 'either through representation or through action'.[13] The break with the reigning thought processes of his time is clear. Myth no longer guides action. It is no longer the story of an archetypal figure. It becomes 'a beam of sentiments related to becoming and being'.[14] This formula, distilled to its essence, may be applied to any myth, that of Telemachus or that of Dionysus. It signals a retreat. In Simondon's analysis, personal mythologies, or the significance of a particular myth in a particular situation, count for little. The content of the myths is secondary. The

---

[13] *Idem*, p. 103.
[14] *Idem*.

essential thing is that the myth connects the individual to the process of becoming. Nevertheless, in the first part of this work, Simondon never mentions the meaning of this connection. He limits himself to describing the 'how'. The sacrifice of meaning was the price to be paid for this Nigredo.

The study of spirituality leads to the same results. Simondon presents the individual as double: he is alone and connected, isolated and part of the collective. This schism within him can be partially resolved through spirituality. Its functional role is to reconnect the individual with his preindividual origin. Spirituality is not another life, and it is not the same life. It is 'the other and the same'.[15] These definitions may seem hollow ... unless they have the profundity of Zen koans. They are typical of Simondon's approach: he affirms the existence of a human spiritual function, and shows that it connects human beings to becoming. Such minimalism is unusual in a philosophical treatise. Simondon rejects creationism, pantheism, and the gamble on eternity. He makes a clean break with all spiritual content. He confines himself to pointing out a vacant space, as one might indicate a vacant chair at the table.

This approach purports to describe individuation, but up until this point it seems to be doing the opposite. Jung, in contrast, borrows elements from a dizzying array of spiritual influences. Mandalas, alchemist engravings, Chinese treatises and zodiac charts support his projections. They are signposts and arrows on a path that leads to a centre indicated by the representations on which he meditates. His individuation is nourished by dreams, objects, drawings. Simondon, for his part, describes individuation in an abstract and general manner. He constructs a formal theory based on the singular, which is another name for the quadrature of the circle.[16] He refrains

---

[15] *Idem*, p. 106.

[16] Translator's note: This is a reference to the classic geometric problem of constructing a square with the same area as a given circle, a task which was proven impossible in the late nineteenth century.

from making particular projections or specific choices, since each determination involves a differentiation. The Nigredo is a process of de-differentiation. The matter over which the alchemist toils is reputed to be neither iron nor copper, nor lead, nor silver, nor any specific substance; and yet it is the essence of all matter. So, too, the individual described by Simondon is an empty form waiting to be truly born.

The unexpected twist occurs half-way through the book. Simondon asserts a distinction: it is necessary to separate individuation from individualization. Individuation is transcendental: it concerns the formal structures of the subject. Kant says of the transcendental that it is valid for every possible consciousness. There is nothing in the transcendental that is empirical or concrete. Individualization, on the other hand, is empirical. It refers to the emergence of the subject according to his life conditions and his temperament. The subject is double: he possesses general structures common to every human being combined with a personal idiosyncracy. His development is guided by these two directions. Simondon does not make reference to the distinction between acquired and innate characteristics, because even that which is innate evolves and is transformed. He asserts that problems belong to the transcendental self. The sense of participating profoundly in the universe, of which the individual is part, itself presents a problem. In contrast, solutions belong to the empirical self who seeks to find a signification for life. The challenge for the 'person' is to unify individuation and individualization: to find adequate answers.

The hardware is mass-produced, the software is personalized ... the connections between technology and individuation begin to emerge. It must first be demonstrated that this distinction between individuation and individualization results in a sharp break with the conception put forth by Jung. For Jung, individuation begins around mid-life. The self cannot be dissolved if it is not yet formed.

Initiations correspond to particular periods of existence. And yet, individuation as conceived by Jung is not a pubescent rite of passage. It does not integrate the individual into a social body; it separates him from it. Dante begins his *Divine Comedy* with these words: '*Nel mezzo del cammin di nostra vita/mi ritrovai per una selva oscura*'. It was in the middle of his life, at the age of 35, that he thought to pay a visit to the country of the dead and the living.

In an article entitled 'Biologie et psychologie analytique (Biology and analytic psychology)', Pierre Solié systematizes Jung's conception. 'From birth until mid-life,' he writes, this is 'the stage dominated by the impulse-driven motor of need and desire, which is almost always mistaken for love. One finds "one's place in the sun", by pushing one's neighbor out of the way, if necessary'.[17] The individual organizes herself around shared signifiers (father, mother, brother, sister, etc.). She experiences the end of the omnipotence of childhood and learns the difference between the self and the object of desire and love. The second part of the article is entitled 'De la mi-vie à la "mort après vie" (From mid-life to "life after death")'. It is during this period that the impulse-driven body attempts to mature into a spiritual body. The Self, the Animus, the Anima, the Shadow, and Individuation, all important Jungian concepts, pertain to this stage. Jung is the psychologist for the over-forty crowd.

Jung describes individuation by following the arrow of time; Simondon describes its structures. He speaks in a formal manner, keeping meaning out of the picture for as long as possible. Individuation is not guided by the identification of an archetype. It is a problem to be resolved: the individual feels herself and knows herself to be double. Extracted from the natural world, of which she is a part, she feels, as a result of her psychological faculties, as if

---

[17] Pierre Solié, 'Biologie et psychologie analytique', in Cahiers de l'Herne, *Jung, op. cit.*, pp. 342–70, p. 349.

she belongs to a different species on this earth. This psychosomatic doubling is the source of the problem. The human being constitutes the union of two 'incomplete symbols of being';[18] this union is 'functional', but its meaning has been lost. A body, a soul: all manner of interpretations are possible. But here, where doctrinarians rush in to explain the marvel that is humanity, Simondon closes the doors. The desire for meaning, however intense it may be, must be sacrificed to the alchemical purgatory of the Nigredo. He rejects the search for meaning through transcendence (God) or through immanence (Nature). 'The quest for transcendence, like the quest for immanence tries to remake the entirety of being using only one of these two symbols of incomplete being which individuation has separated'.[19] The only thing which must be taken into account, according to Simondon, is the existence of a 'complete' reality *prior to* individuation. And yet, neither immanence nor transcendence does take this reality into account. Simondon repudiates materialism, which seeks to find the essence of being within the physical body. He also rejects the idea of the soul, that spiritualization of the conscience.

The only true monism, explains Simondon, must be generative. It consists of seizing 'the unity' at the moment when the first hint of potential for a diversity of structures and operations surfaces. 'The only true monism is that which, rather than following an implicit dualism which it seems to reject, contains within itself the dimension of a possible dualism, but on a foundation of being which cannot slip away'.[20] This is the dream of a creator.... To be in attendance at the Big Bang.... The first operation.... To see oneself being born while watching the birth of worlds arising out of the ether. All of Simondon's philosophy is concerned with genesis. Yet he rejects the notion of creation. And 'unfortunately, it is impossible for the human

[18] *Individuation psychique et collective*, p. 137.
[19] *Idem.*
[20] *Idem*, p. 142.

subject to witness his own genesis'.[21] For this reason, meaning must be sought instead in a process that mimics creation: invention.

The meaning of individuation: The relation to the object

After a critique of adaptation and diversion, both of which are social relationships in which the individual is forgotten, Simondon goes in search of an authentic experience. He finds this experience in the trans-individual, a relation with the other and with the universe which brings to its subject 'a dimension of eternity'.[22] Wisdom, heroism and saintliness are three figures which epitomize the trans-individual. It is at the level of the trans-idividual that spiritual meanings may be discovered.[23] In this relation, the individual surpasses his limits. He is outside himself, overwhelmed, ecstatic in the presence of the other. Simondon speaks of experience. From the preindividual there arises: a shared emotion, a sense of belonging, a sense of otherness, love.

And then there is technology. This transition from human relationships to the world of objects is, perhaps, abrupt, but it is in the spirit of Simondon's philosophy. There is one mode of trans-individualism to which he ascribes a special significance: the relation between the individual and the object. Simondon's quest for meaning leads him at last to technology, which he elevates to the highest level of relationship that the individual can experience. The last five pages of his *Individuation psychique et collective* attest to this, in a series of passages that constitute one of his most original contributions to philosophical thought. These pages speak of the 'consequences of the notion of individuation': alongside love, the other and spirituality, Simondon summons the object. In the iron and steel workings of the

---

[21] *Idem*, p. 163.
[22] *Idem*, p. 158.
[23] *Idem*, p. 196.

machine, he finds gold. Is this not the realization of the alchemist's defining goal?

Here, Simondon differentiates himself. After his lengthy negation of singular contents and specific significations, he makes a decisive choice in favour of technology. The paradoxical advantage of this choice is that technology has no specific content. It is neutral. It transcends communities, those groupings of human beings who share the same values. Communities look for stability. Neophobes – those who fear and resist innovation – judge between 'good' and 'bad'. In contrast, open societies – those that favour and give rise to technological invention – seek expansion. They are beyond the duality of good and bad: they experience 'an infinite continuity of gradations of value, from nothingness to perfection'.[24] The technician judges between the irrelevant and the constructive, the neutral and the positive. He pursues individuation: he opens up the process of becoming without confining it to a particular signification.

Simondon speaks of the technical operation as a 'condition of individuation'.[25] He defines it in terms of seven parameters, which correspond to the expectations he had formulated in his search for the meaning of individuation. (1) Technology (like individuation) can always go further; (2) the relationship with the object can bypass social mediation (this mediation handicaps the individual by obliging her to adapt); (3) 'the technician cannot do otherwise than to act freely';[26] (4) technology is stronger than the values of communities, which must be modified on its account; (5) technology 'institutes a transindividual relation from one individual to another that develops without reference to any communal integration guaranteed by a collective mythology';[27] (6) technology creates a civilization; (7)

---

[24] *Idem*, p. 259.
[25] *Idem*, p. 263.
[26] *Idem*, p. 264.
[27] *Idem*, p. 266.

the technical being is 'the correlative of the self-creation of the individual':[28] it is the *alter techno*.

This technology is, in part, a fantasy. Simondon draws from his personal mythology. Individuation leads to an archetype: a 'pure individual'.[29] The technician is such an individual. 'In a community, he seems to belong to a different species'.[30] He is subject to different obligations and different prohibitions because his function is not directly assigned by the group, but is rather the result of a skill. Like the doctor, technician of the healing arts, like 'the sorcerer and the preacher',[31] the technician is in a relationship with unfamiliar forces. He is engaged in a solitary dialogue with an opaque world. He brings to the group something new and irreplaceable. The technician does not work: the mediation he exercises between the community and an object hidden from view does not fit within an established social framework. He is a seeker; he illuminates zones of obscurity. This activity liberates him from the yoke of social obligation: 'liberated individuals', declares Simondon, 'are those who conduct research, and through this search establish a non-social relation with the object'.[32] The collective mythology has no further hold on these individuals, since invention is their source of fulfilment. Should we consider the technician an egotist? No more so than a painter or a poet, counters Simondon, since they are also seekers at the outskirts of society. But when the discoveries in question consist of technical objects, they are viewed with a suspicious eye by a society that wants above all to plunge into the 'hypnotic state'[33] which is achieved through the possession of a device sanctioned by societal propaganda: 'Art of façade and sleight of hand'![34] The human taste

[28] *Idem*, p. 267.
[29] *Idem*, p. 261.
[30] *Idem*.
[31] *Idem*.
[32] *Idem*, p. 263.
[33] *Idem*, p. 281.
[34] *Idem*.

for technology has been corrupted[35] – preoccupied with pleasure, scornful of authenticity. In Simondon's words there is an element of Rousseau-ism applied to the human relationship with technology.

The *terrae incognitae* of ancient geographical maps were thoroughly trampled across by the heroes of Jules Verne stories. Hot-air balloons, ships, rockets and submarines turn the world into a launching pad towards certain key points within a world hidden from view. The earth itself is criss-crossed with passages and openings through which to access them. Whether they consist of mine shafts, volcanic craters, cracks in the ocean floor or subterranean laboratories, there is always a place where the voyage begins, a place inaccessible to the community at large. When Simondon noted that he was inspired by Verne,[36] rather than by other philosophers to elaborate his philosophy of technology, he was referring not so much to the machines Verne described, in spite of the ingeniousness of their conception, but to the radical nature of the break with society that the voyage entails. Societal values fade away before the spectacle of cities held aloft on mineral peaks. And from the peaceful depths explored by Captain Nemo, the petty machinations of the world above seem like vain agitations. Nemo's defiance is legendary. His quest is one of non-participation in the society from which technology shields him, propelled beneath the oceanic depths that envelope him in silence.

Simondon is another of these explorers of limits – these indefatigable, uncompromising purists. And it is as if there were two

---

[35] *Idem*, p. 280.

[36] *Entretien sur la mécanologie* (*Interview on mechanical thought*) with Jean Le Moyne. In response to the question 'Do you recognize the existence of a mechanically minded current of thought, beginning, perhaps, with Reuleaux?', Simondon replies as follows: 'Yes ... I don't know very much about the authors that you have been kind enough to bring to my attention ... but there is a mechanical-mindedness that exists, at the very least as a preference, a tendency, and in the poetry of the relationship between the most perfect industry, or the most well-equipped science, and nature in its most natural state, that is to say, the most spontaneous and the least marred by human influence. In France, for example, Jules Verne represents this tendency; my passion for mechanical things owes more to Jules Verne's futuristic novels, written in the nineteenth century, than it does to any actual philosophers, technicians, or mechanical specialists.'

technologies: one that spurs us to travel and one that is used for travelling. The first is a cutting-edge technology, not because of its sophistication or advanced automatism – these are mere distractions, since the wheel is no less a product of technology than is the laser – but rather, because of its individuating effect. If technologies inspire exploration, it is because they mobilize contemplation, intelligence and fantasy. An affinity for the gestures of technology fuels an imagination in which gesture serves as technician. Is this a will to power? In the Nietzschean sense, perhaps, since neither wealth nor political power come into play. Cutting-edge technologies, in Simondon's conception, are so far removed from any social or political applications that theirs is less a will to power than a power derived from dreams.

Next, there is the second class of technologies: those with which we travel. Volkswagen, cars for the people, all the more trustworthy for the fact that their technological nature is so little in evidence. They have become *genera*, according to the expression used in Roman law. Socially, they have joined the ranks of mediators, of means towards an end, they have become travel itself, since it is in this capacity that they are relevant to the lives of city-dwellers. They become the vehicles of desire, implicit and explicit, so much so that their technical nature becomes merely one element in a larger context. 'We have had the opportunity to see,' writes Simondon, 'a female student driving a car on the occasion of a group excursion, who deliberately brutalizes the clutch pedal and the gear shifter, in order to provide her male comrades with a demonstration of objectified femininity.' So much for the game of seduction.

Rebirth of an archetype

It is striking to note that Robinson Crusoe was able to recreate on his island a material setting analogous to that of the England he had left behind, thanks to the carpenter's trunk and other materials salvaged from the wreck. If today a shipwrecked castaway were to find himself in possession of the equipment of a merchant ship, it would be useless to him. His environment would better support the technologies of the eighteenth century. Gestures are no longer sufficient when our technologies are not mechanical tools but black boxes. We can imitate a carpenter, not an electronics expert. The black box is impenetrable in the absence of an energy source and a specific knowledge of the procedures by which it functions. Today's technology is controlled indirectly. The object becomes the measure of all things, and since the object is opaque, the measurements are lost.

Simondon reactivated an archetype. Even in the 1960s he sensed that the situation was perilous. He saw the empire of an 'ethics of returns'[37] and its effects on the educational system and on every other front. Work, reduced to tiny increments, was divorced from all purpose or meaning. He saw what was demanded of technology: telephones worked, but no one knew how. Contentment as long as the car runs smoothly, frustration when it breaks down; this is the syndrome of the sorcerer's apprentice. Simondon saw the birth of a new and irreversible form of idiocy. This idiocy is not mitigated by the extenuating circumstances of unconsciousness. It is a proud and wilful stupidity that knowingly wastes, pollutes and destroys. Never has humanity been so far removed from the earth and from the animal world. Never have human beings been less concerned with the legacy they were leaving for their descendants. Discussions of sustainable development are a symptom. Just as a man in good health celebrates his good fortune by planning a trip to the North Pole and not by discussing his physical condition, a generation that was doing its utmost to ensure its continued endurance would never

---

[37] *Individuation psychique et collective*, p. 288.

have thought to come up with a concept as absurd as 'sustainable development'. It's like talking about an especially round circle!

The exclamation 'They don't realize!' has an immediate practical effect: it causes anyone who hears it to flee. Especially when it is true. For Jung, as we have noted, individuation begins with isolation and is accompanied by a feeling of culpability. Given the acuteness of his sensitivity to the problems that afflict technological societies, Simondon himself may well have had a first-hand experience of these feelings. The passages in his book concerning anguish and solitude take on a personal tone. And yet, Jung also notes that this feeling of culpability can be mitigated by the positive values that the individual brings back to society. This theme preoccupied Simondon, all the more so, since he saw the limitations of the two classic solutions to the crises that arise within a technological society: romanticism and capitalism. Romanticism advocates a return to nature and to a subsistence economy. This is equivalent to throwing the baby out with the bath water, all the more so because, while a subsistence economy may be viable for a population of one billion, it is not at all clear that this would still be the case for a population six or even ten times larger. Capitalism counts on the self-regulating nature of the market-place. Its apparent 'cynicism' is really a calculated logic. If problems become too great, it is in the interest of the market to resolve them. But logic is not commensurate with conscience. Furthermore, in Simondon's view, the ethics of returns is in large part responsible for the crisis it purports to resolve: it is a source of enslavement.

Mentalities are partially to blame. The problem is, first of all, psychological. Western rationality has dissociated the object from the subject. This approach is necessary to the development of science, but in the practical domain it results in a dualistic mentality. The intimate relationship that exists between the mechanic and his motorcycle or the vintner and her wine is disrupted. The subject's sense of responsibility is diminished; the object is left to fend for itself. The subject is preoccupied with his ego, never realizing that it is the product of his actions. Technical objects are the materialization of human intentions. When these intentions are no longer understood, the objects become irrelevant. We treat them like pebbles. But our indifference towards the technical object is also an indifference towards a part of ourselves. It is the quality of the relationship that matters. Simondon has great esteem for the artisanal mentality: it represents a warm relationship.

A sense of quality is essential to our piece of mind. It defies explanation. Quality is not something rational, but something felt. It comes with experience; it is transmitted in a gesture, a glance. It is a sort of *savoir-faire*, a vocation, a feeling of responsibility for oneself and for the other: a consciousness, since it originates in the human mind and not in the object. 'The real cycle you're working on is a cycle called yourself', writes Robert Pirsig in *Zen and the Art of Motorcycle Maintenance*, a book that is Simondonian from start to finish. Riding through the mountains of Montana, the hero of this *bildungsroman* shares his reflections on motorcycles and on technology. He explains that the motorcycle is a mental phenomenon. Its steel parts have no inherent form; it is the human mind that turns them into a functional system. Anyone who understands this will not feel the need to purchase a new motorcycle each year. The motorcycle will no longer be, in Simondon's terms, a 'social adornment (*parure sociale*)'. It will no longer have the aura of a magical object upon which we impose our demands and expectations. It will become a motorcycle with which we can forge a connection, and this connection, according to Persig, is what gives shape to our journeys across Montana.

Quality can become a source of obsession. There is a certain madness attached to this intangible concept. Pirsig's hero is plunged into a period of schizophrenia as a result of his attempts to rationalize the concept of quality. But quality is inherently at odds with rationality. It is a spirit, an attitude, an *intuition*. Like a gesture, it can be learned, but not thought. According to Pirsig, the problems associated with technologies arise from the fact that they are inevitably viewed through the lens of rationality:

> [T]he real evil isn't the objects of technology but the tendency of technology to isolate people into lonely attitudes of objectivity. It's the objectivity, the dualistic way of looking at things underlying technology, that produces the evil. That's why I went to so much trouble to show how technology could be used to destroy the evil. A person who knows how to fix motorcycles ... with Quality ... is less likely to run short of friends than one who doesn't. And they aren't going to see him as some kind of object either. Quality destroys objectivity every time.[38]

The archetype of the intuitive technician has always inhabited our collective unconscious. It has fed our collective imagination since the dawn of time. In using this imagination to explore the physical and generative boundaries of reality, Simondon's work on individuation brought the archetype into the realm of conscious awareness. This is not the least of his accomplishments.

[38] R. Pirsig, *Zen and the Art of Motorcycle Maintenance*, New York: William Morrow & Co, 1974, p. 322.

11

An Ideal World

Progress may be envisaged in two ways: a comparative sense and a superlative sense. In the comparative sense, two states of being or two situations are evaluated. In the superlative sense, an entire series of states is taken into consideration and compared to an ideal which is to be the culmination of progress. This superlative is the goal that gives direction to a series of successive steps. For many philosophers, progress is a comparative for which the superlative does not exist. There is a sense of movement forward, but the direction is imprecise, opaque, unknown. Suppositions on this topic tend to take the form of projections rather than predictions. We avoid assigning an end state to progress so as not to constrain its trajectory; the surprises it has in store invariably render all imagined outcomes laughable.

Simondon's strength is his ability to think of progress from both perspectives. His philosophy is driven by finalism. He wants to encourage forward movement. An absence of direction is painful to him. Influenced by Descartes, he takes the position that reason must assign itself goals, and that these goals must be reflected in its output. Otherwise, it becomes unfocused and distracted. 'So blind is the curiosity by which mortals are possessed,' wrote Descartes, 'that they often conduct their minds along unexplored routes, having no reason to hope for success, but merely being willing to risk the experiment of finding whether the truth they seek lies there.'[1] They burn with the mad desire to discover a treasure, without knowing what the treasure is or where to look for it. They search, therefore, at random. The Cartesian method consists of setting reason back on the right track; likewise, Simondon has tracks, and trains, in mind.

Simondon turned himself into a historian of technologies in order to describe their progress in a comparative manner. He compared the stages of development in order to demonstrate that technical objects tend towards concreteness. Modern telephones are more concrete than the telephones of the 1960s. They have an independent energy source and a stored memory. They are more coherent. They perform a wider range of functions. Simondon traced the lineage of numerous technical objects in order to piece together a schema of evolution. He investigated the genealogies of families of motors, batteries and aeroplanes. This technological taxonomy led him to conclude that an object that evolves successfully will be better integrated than its predecessors. It will form a whole. The vestiges of intellectual projection will have disappeared. The material will be organized in an optimal way, in order to execute the functions for which it is intended. The object will be smaller and lighter. Through its evolution it becomes simpler. The number of pieces it contains, its response time, and sometimes even its price, decrease. Its technological function is perfected.

At times, the lines of concretization reach an end. We have previously noted that the shape of church bells has not evolved since the twelfth century. They fulfil their function perfectly, since theirs is the most economical structure possible. Computer calculations have independently confirmed that the ideal form for a bell corresponds exactly to the classic shape. Progress has already

---

[1] Descartes, 'Rules for the direction of the mind' (*Règles pour la direction de l'esprit*), in *The Philosophical Writings of Descartes*, Vol. 1, trans. John Cottingham, Cambridge: Cambridge University Press, 1985, p. 15.

reached its fullest expression. This is to say that a comparative perspective can lead to the identification of a superlative. Should we therefore consider that a finality can be identified within the evolution of technologies? Does the optimum form towards which these technical lineages develop also correspond to the superlative of progress? To answer these questions in the affirmative would be to overlook invention, which is the beginning of a new lineage that branches out from the established paths. Computer science has arrived at an advanced degree of development, but with the new connections being forged between computer science and biology the game is still in play. What constitutes an optimum form for one evolutionary trajectory may not be optimal for another. In this sense, the comparative perspective is purely descriptive. It does not culminate in any single finality, because the logic by which it operates is infinite.

The superlative of progress

The nature of the superlative of progress is a question for general philosophy. It consists of defining an intention and an ideal. In order to ask these types of questions, we must depart from our description of technical lineages. Empricism is no longer sufficient: the idea cannot be the result of a collection of facts; the intention is not the sum of all enquiries. The question of superlatives belongs to metaphysics. This is why it has gone out of fashion. There are all manner of specific philosophies: a philosophy of contemporary art, a philosophy of genetics, a philosophy of history, or even of cooking. But there is no longer a philosophy of everything. Philosophy approaches a million different subjects without addressing that unwieldy object which contains all the others: the universe. Every thing is significant, but not *everything*.

In a text cited by William James at the beginning of his *Pragmatism*, Chesterton expressed amazement that philosophy could neglect this important question:

> But there are some people, nevertheless – and I am one of them – who think that the most practical and important thing about a man is still his view of the universe. We think that for a landlady considering a lodger, it is important to know his income, but still more important to know his philosophy. We think that for a general about to fight an enemy, it is important to know the enemy's numbers, but still more important to know the enemy's philosophy. We think the question is not whether the theory of the cosmos affects matters, but whether in the long run, anything else affects them.[2]

This opinion is shared by Simondon. In the last section of his *Mode d'existence d'objets techniques*, he provides his vision of the history of the universe. He speaks of the place of religions and technologies, of science and ethics. He traces their origins and anticipates their destination. This is the least read portion of Simondon's book. It is wide-ranging, sometimes mythic. Its reconstitution of the story of humanity shows signs of a Hegelian influence. A Gnostic enthusiasm fortifies his confidence in his capacity to predict the direction in which humanity is headed. Simondon placed these pages at the summit of his oeuvre. They contain the description of a progress towards the superlative.

In the beginning, there was magic. This word designates the harmonious and purposeful existence of humanity in earliest times. This magic is not a collection of superstitions, incantations or paranormal activity. It is an experience in which human beings are not distant from the world. They participate in it. Their actions have an effect upon the cosmos, just as the world acts upon them.

---

[2] G.K. Chesterton, *The Heretics*, New York: John Lane Co, 1905, pp. 15–16.

Our mental categories are ill suited to understanding what Simondon refers to as 'magic'. We separate object from subject, figure from background, the whole from its parts. Our lives are structured around the distinction between reason and intuition, left brain and right brain. Magic designates the ideal moment that preceded these separations. It is a state of completeness.

In the magical system, the earth, or the mountain, or the valley, or the ocean, is connected to that which is singular and precise in an experience (for example, a particular gesture, word or action). A word has an effect on the world. The Indian who chants incantations at sunrise experiences a relation between his incantations and the rising sun. In this example, analytic reason would certainly dissociate a culturally specific rite from an astrological law. But in the magical experience, human gestures are linked with the natural world by a network of key points and key moments. The Indian is acting in such a place at such a moment. There are cardinal points in space and exceptional moments in time. If there is an exchange between human rites and the entire cosmos, it passes by way of this spatio-temporal network of points and moments.[3]

But just as the Golden Age came to an end, the magical unity split apart. Simondon explains that the magic 'shifted its phase'. By this, he means that the two types of reality which the magic had

---

[3] Simondon locates this structuring in certain exceptional acts: 'Ascent, exploration, and more generally, any pioneering gesture demonstrate adherence to the key points that nature presents. To ascend a slope toward the summit is to make one's way toward the privileged place that commands the entire mountain range, not in order to dominate or possess it, but to exchange with it a relation of friendship. Man and nature are not, strictly speaking, enemies before that adhesion to the key point, but they are strangers to one another. As long as it has not been ascended, the summit is simply a summit, a location higher than others. The ascent gives it the character of a fuller, richer place, no longer abstract, in which this exchange between man and world takes place. ... An expedition or a navigation that allow us to reach a new continent by a defined route does not conquer anything; and yet, they are valid for magical thought, because they put us in contact with this continent in a privileged place that constitutes a key point (*point-clé*). The magical universe is made of a network of access points opening onto each domain of reality: these consist of thresholds, summits, limits, crossing points, attached to one another by their singularity and their exceptional character' (*Mode d'existence*, p. 166).

kept in harmony were no longer in sync. From this disjunction there arose two separate ways of relating to the world. The first preserved the localized, fragmented and segmented aspect of the primitive magic. It corresponds to the *technical* experience, that is, to physical manipulations, actions and gestures. It is fundamentally limited and precise. For technology, the global relation with the world is of little importance. Technology separates and analyses. Its ambition does not go beyond the localized context in which it acts. It is efficient, but without universal impact. The other way of relating to the world inherits the fundamental, cosmic dimension of the magic. It becomes *religion*, that is, the experience of active influences and capabilities. It is universal, but it has lost the sense of the singular and the local. It cannot conceive of concrete action, except by putting it in relation with the whole. Technology has no sense of totality. Religion has no sense of the singular.

Neither the gestures nor the cosmic dimension of the magic have been lost. Only the relation between the gesture and the cosmos is lacking. In a sense, the Indian is still there, with his incantations and ritual technologies. And the sun also rises. But the magical charge has faded, because there is no longer anything that connects the two dimensions. The *centre* had been between the gesture and the cosmos; it was a relation. After the magic shifted its phase, it was as if there were two centres, one a centre of physical manipulation and control, around which all technical things were assembled, and the other a centre of contemplation, which served as a rallying point for all religious and spiritual experiences.

The story which Simondon recounts has numerous ramifications. In a general manner, it is marked by a force of union and a force of separation. Both art and philosophy are engaged in attempts at reunion. Art is sometimes able to re-establish communication between the limited aspect of things and their adherence to a wider-ranging reality. Philosophy is, for Simondon, an institution of relations. The philosopher's task is to reunite the elements that other activities, which are always in some way unilateral, drive apart. Separation, the second force at play in this history, is essentially the consequence of monolithic activities, either because they are too analytical, too segmented and too technical, or because they have lost contact with the variety of the concrete by settling themselves in the universal. For example, pragmatic ethics is too technical, because it presents itself as a set of prescriptions for action. Conversely, the Kantian ethics of the categorical imperative is too exaggerated in its desire for the universal: it minimizes the importance of specific circumstances and conditions.

Simondon manifests his confidence in this history by anticipating the end of philosophy. He longs for a new basis for creating relations. Wisdom, for him, is a way of living and thinking that could unite the technical and the religious, the finite and the infinite, and could reconcile the coexistence of opposites. A bit of magic might also help.

True progress would be a reconciliation. The superlative towards which we strive is behind us. The magic that existed before the separation represents the ideal we seek to retrieve. The end of times will mirror the beginning. History comes full circle; the interplay of the forces of separation and union must resolve at last into a re-established harmony. Simondon's philosophy is fundamentally optimistic. Those people of good will who work to piece back together the fragments of the broken vase will ultimately reverse the fatality of the fall. This philosophy is also ahistorical.... It anticipates a final state of things that will constitute a time outside of time, a departure from history. At that point, 'progress' will have lost all meaning: the real and the ideal will have merged.[4]

---

[4] Gilbert Hottois observed the change in Simondon's philosophical orientation in the third part of the *Mode d'existence*: 'It is all a matter of thought and recuperation, by means of (philosophical) thought, of the dissociations (of prephilosophical thought: existentially lived, become) from that magical, coalescent childhood. The real world of technology and its specific potentialities, its irreducible specificity, moves into the

This mythical projection allows us to evaluate progress. There is no real forward motion unless the relations between humanity and the world are favoured. In this sense, the technological progress which Simondon seeks to vindicate is reinterpreted as a false progress. It is more truly a 'regress', and a regrettable one at that, since it signifies a loss of harmony. In the comparative sense, technological progress is positive. The technical lineages evolve towards greater concretization. But when this progress is placed in the context of the ensemble of human activities, it appears to be a regression. It is too specialized. Nothing tempers the exclusively analytic aspect of technologies. They have lost their sense of the world. Their actions are carried out with indifference. They are neutral, 'detached',[5] says Simondon. The technical object is not part of the world. It is distinguished from the natural object in that it is an additional object, introduced into the milieu as a result of human will. It is a fragment capable of operating in any situation or location, but it is outside the jurisdiction of natural law. It is a materialization of freedom: a product of nature that transcends its natural origins.

The problem of technology may be interpreted in terms of the relationship between freedom and nature. If we translate the 'human adventure' as Simondon presents it with the aid of this mythological vocabulary, we find the following: in the beginning there was nature;

background. The resistance of the techno-scientific dynamic to its own recuperation by philosophical thought, which is at the heart of all that ails civilization, has dwindled to the point of disappearing without a trace. There lies the weak spot, or the limit: as analogical-speculative thought becomes autonomous and gains confidence, the reference to the real, to its resistance, its independence, its otherness, which had set this thought in motion in the first place, is lost. Very strong at the beginning of the *Mode d'existence...*, it has been sublimated, volatilized, so that by the end, there's nothing but thinking, thinking about ways of thinking, thinking in an ecumenical sense.' Hottois speaks of a philosophical irenicism, which he explains as follows: 'A certain angelic do-gooder-ism characterizes the temptation specific to Simondonian philosophy to heal symbolically with thought', in G. Hottois, *Simondon et la philosophie de la 'culture technique'*, op. cit., pp. 124–5. Simondon: *une technique angélique?* (Simondon: an angelic technology?).

[5] *Mode d'existence*, p. 172.

freedom, which is an intrinsic part of nature, detached itself and created technical objects. These objects belong to nature, because nature is all-encompassing, but they do not obey its laws. In the same way, freedom is natural and also supernatural, immanent and transcendent. But rather than consecrating a set of laws specific to technology, thus liberating technologies from natural law (which is the current trend), Simondon goes against the current. He argues for a new connection between nature and freedom. The eschatology of his myth presents a freedom which would return to nature. There exists, in sum, a natural law or at least a 'harmony' of the world which technologies must find their way back to, or else be condemned to remain suspended in a second world which would be impoverished, since it would preserve no vestige of its origins. Technical progress is a necessary *hubris*. Real progress is a reformed, that is to say philosophical, *hubris*.

This way of seeing things can have practical results. The ecologist movement, the pleas for 'green industry' and for recyclable, non-polluting technologies attest to a will to reunite technology and nature. Post-industrial societies have become aware of the effects of their way of life upon the equilibrium of the planet. The theme of the integrity of nature demonstrates the resurgence of longing for harmony. Simondon is in tune with certain environmentalist advocates of the present day.

Technologies, sacred and profane (Eliade and Simondon)

Nevertheless, three years after the publication of his *Mode d'existence des objets techniques*, Simondon revised his analysis. He taught a course at the Sorbonne entitled 'Psycho-sociologie de la technicité (Psycho-sociology of technology)'. In this course he addressed a peculiar problem, which prompted him to reframe his conception of progress: the connections between technology and the sacred. The importance of the theme of sacredness in Simondon's philosophy has not been sufficiently highlighted. We automatically expect a philosopher of technologies to favour the canon of modern reason. But Simondon's case is more complex. One part of his philosophy is closely aligned with Descartes, but he was also influenced by other authors considered marginal by the university hierarchy: Jung and Eliade. His ideas concerning spirituality are heavily influenced by the philosophy of Meister Eckhart. In a note concerning his travels to India he makes reference to the practice of yoga. Ancient practices and ancient wisdom modified the way in which he viewed technology.

The connections between technology and the sacred are ancient and indissoluble. These connections were lost from view in the modern era, which believed itself to have severed the links between technology and the sacred in favour of a closer association between technology and science. But originally, these two domains were not so distinct. For 'archaic' societies, almost every aspect of life was in some way connected to the sacred. As Eliade notes:

> One of the most embarrassing difficulties for the historian of religions is that the nearer he approaches to 'origins,' the greater becomes the number of 'religious facts.' This is so much so that in certain cases (for example, in archaic or prehistoric societies) one asks himself what is not or has not once been 'sacred' or connected with the sacred.[6]

Yoga is a breathing technique and a source of wisdom. In the ancient Roman religion, the ploughing, the harvests and the plantings were as sacred as any technique. These fundamental actions were ritualized. They were accompanied by auspices, sacrifices and festivals. Simondon also evokes Eliade's book *The Forge and the Crucible* (*Forgerons et alchimistes*). The blacksmith's work with molten metal turns him into

---

[6] Eliade, *La nostalgie des origines*, Paris: Gallimard, 1978; translated as *The Quest: History and Meaning in Religion*, Chicago: University of Chicago Press, 1969, p. 68.

a being half-god, half-demon, and a hero of civilization. Alchemy consecrates the link between a material oeuvre and a process of spiritual regeneration. These examples shed light on the harmony of origins: the domains are not separate. The division of labour exists, but it does not imply a division of mentalities. The technical spirit is not resistant to the sacred or vice versa.

What is the present situation, asks Simondon? His first response, analysed above, is to observe that there has been a divorce. But in his course on the psycho-sociology of technology, he defends a different thesis: there exists an 'isomorphism' between sacredness (*sacralité*) and technology (*technicité*). Simondon's choice of terminology indicates that he is considering the 'form' or the 'structure' of the sacred, and that he sees a commonality with the form of technology. As a structuralist, he leaves aside the content of the sacred experience. He does not address the numinous character, the *mysterium fascinans et tremendum* (the mystery that both attracts and repels) which is specific to a sacred reality. Technology also has an aspect at once fascinating and repellent. But Simondon's analysis is focused on the structure of the world that permits magical thinking. This structure may be perceived in the existence of privileged moments and central locations. Eliade, whose analyses are frequently cited by Simondon, tells us that a sacred location constitutes 'a break in the homogeneity of space'.[7] The temple, the sanctuary or the sacred mountain have a quality that sets them apart from neighbouring realities. They are at the centre of the world. For traditional peoples this is more than a conviction: it is a certainty without which they could not live. The Achilpa, Australian nomads, have a sacred pole which is the cosmic axis, the axis mundi. They plant it in the ground each time they set up camp. The chaos of a wild region becomes a world that has a centre

[7] Eliade, *The Sacred and the Profane*, trans.Willard R. Trask, Orlando, FL: Harcourt, 1959, p. 37.

and thus a meaning. According to a myth, the sacred pole once broke. The entire tribe was overcome with anguish. Its members wandered aimlessly for a time, until finally they lay down on the ground to allow death to claim them.

Within the cycle of time there are also privileged moments. The return of the new year, the rituals of regeneration and the repetition of cosmogonies were moments in which archaic peoples were removed from profane or secular time and plunged into a 'dream time'. Myth plucks man from his own time, a time that is individual, chronological, historical. It projects him symbolically into a circular time whose origin is the absolute. The myth that Simondon presents at the end of *Mode d'existence des objets techniques* serves the same function. It recalls the experience of a Golden Age and a longing for its return. The sacred world is a network of key points and key moments. Human beings and their symbols respond to one another. Meaning is born from the possibility of interpreting nature and existence through myth. Everything is connected, everything is in communication.

At first glance, the technological vision of the world seems diametrically opposed to this type of experience. The technical object is connected to that which is near to it. It is separated from the whole. Analytical reason has undermined the coherence of a system that had been united. However, says Simondon, by way of a corrective for his earlier analyses, this is only true of industrial objects. These objects are closed off, isolated, like an oven or a steam-engine, but technologies have moved beyond this isolation. They are organized into networks. Each technical object becomes a terminal. From this point on, essential activities are centred on relayed communications and remotely controlled actions, which suppose the existence of a centre or centres, privileged points, zones of influence. In a portrait worthy of Jules Verne teleported to the 1960s, Simondon evokes the inaugural act of a rocket launch: Cape Canaveral has become the centre of the world. Aeroplanes, he writes, must be considered in the context of their relation with aerodromes, radio navigation networks and supply systems. A new ecumenicalism appears with technology: an ecumenicalism based on fact, more solid than the 'precarious ecumenicalism'[8] of religions, says Simondon. The entire planet is calibrated to Greenwich Mean Time; radio waves are not the province of any specific group, and the potential for growth, he says, is 'virtually infinite'. How his thesis would have been bolstered had he lived to see contemporary laboratories and their research on living things!

Technology creates a world. Its impact is cosmic, like that of the sacred. Like the sacred experience, it organizes this world by creating centres within it, privileged points and moments.[9] The central figure in ancient thought also has an analogue in the world of technology. "the high priest who performs these new rites," writes Simondon, 'is the man in the white coat; his creed is Research. Like the priest, he is ascetic and sometimes singular'.[10]

It is difficult to say whether this analysis is a description or a projection, an observation or a desire. Here, the status of technology is altered. It had been a limited activity, with no connection to the whole. It acted in a localized and specific manner. It became the analogue of the sacred, which signifies that it is reconnected with the whole. It is a network grafted on to nature; that is, a 'second nature' which is the superlative of progress, the Simondonian ideal. Does the author mean to say that technology is a substitute for the sacred,

---

[8] Simondon, *Psycho-sociologie de la technicité*, p. 342.
[9] In an echo of the bells we heard earlier: 'The bell-tower is no more essentially tied to the church than a radio antenna; it simply corresponds to a more primitive means of transmitting information. A similarity in function (propagating radiating energy, whether mechanical or electromagnetic, over long distances) leads to a similarity of material structures, and thus to a virtual isomorphism: any bell-tower could be repurposed as a radio wave transmitter, without modification, as if it had been constructed for that very purpose', in *idem*, p. 331.
[10] *Idem*, p. 345.

that it eliminates and replaces an earlier spirituality? No. These two experiences have the same organization, but different content. The sacred and the technical conflict with one another at the level of intentions.

The sacred sets its sights on the unique and the irreplaceable. Having lost their sacred pole, the Achilpa waited for death. Nothing could serve as a substitute. For the sacred the norm has already been given. Either it remains or it is lost. This way of thinking recognizes two values: the sacred and the profane. It does not recognize lukewarm mixtures or half-measures. It has the sense of something given and the value of its integrity. The minds of technicians conceive of things quite differently: for them, the norms were never given. They are yet to be discovered. There is no such thing as uniqueness. The technician finds substitutes, makes copies, adds improvements. Technology has an infinite number of values. Its products are transitory, subject to amelioration. It thrives on invention, an activity which sacred thought considers tantamount to a break with the cosmic order.

Simondon is in search of balance. He cares about justice. Real progress, which is also the ideal of progress, would be achieved through a convergence of technology and the sacred. Simondon seeks to find, for contemporary technologies, the ancient connections between technology and the sacred. He is in search of a value shared between them, even as their very contents seem irreconcilable. This value would not belong to the domain of ethics, which can never be made universal. Certainly, Simondon himself developed a code of ethics in the final pages of his *Individuation psychique et collective*, but in the final analysis this code amounts to an aesthetic: the purpose of an action is to integrate harmoniously with life. Simondon's ethics is an ethics of becoming. It navigates between two obstacles: the isolated act, connected only to itself, and the act that would become absolute. This ethics is the search for a resonance, the tension that maintains a fair relationship. It is shaped by the ideal of the network: each act must be coordinated with the other acts. This is not an ethical principle but a privilege accorded to those whose resonance connects with something beyond themselves.

The technoaesthetic

The encounter between the sacred and the technical will be realized through a new aesthetics. Simondon is guided by a sense of beauty. He uses the word 'technoaesthetic' in a letter to Derrida,[11] explaining his taste for objects and situations that combine elements of nature with human activity: a musical instrument, a boat blown by the wind. He perceives beauty in a tool adapted to its function. The gesture of loosening a jammed screw can be 'orgasmic'.[12] Le Corbusier, Xenakis and Léger are among the artist-technicians whose work most appeals to him. Their aesthetic is neither baroque nor over-ornate. It is analytical, functional. The forms these artists create are not applied to matter in an arbitrary fashion. They follow the texture of the materials used: the veins of a rock, the folds of the metal removed from the rolling machine. The technical gesture is not hidden. Le Corbusier shows the pipes, the metal bars within the concrete. He provides passageways for energy forms that don't yet exist. He attempts to connect geometry and nature.[13]

This sensibility is the foundation of Simondon's philosophy. It furnishes him with images, intuitions. It gives his work a singular tone. Simondon has a way of sensing and perceiving that is rare among intellectuals. In his eyes, 'we lack technical poets'.[14] He is

[11] This uncompleted letter is reproduced in the journal *Papiers du Collège International de Philosophie*, no. 12, 1992.

[12] *Idem.*

[13] On Le Corbusier, cf. *Imagination et invention*, p. 992.

[14] Unpublished text on mechanology.

looking for words to describe the experience of a beauty linked to action.

The technoaesthetic is not contemplative. It is sensitive to transformations and mutations. It thrives on change. The successful completion of a difficult mechanical operation is a source of pleasure. Amateur watchmakers and locksmiths can attest to this. Builders also. But the technoaesthetic goes beyond technology. Simondon also sees it in operation in physics, biology and psychology. His philosophy is oriented towards processes. The individuation of the crystal or the metamorphosis of the butterfly inspire the same sentiment of beauty. The technoaesthetic is a contemplation of action. It is reflected in the gleaming eyes of the artist-technician who delights in the emergence of a natural or artificial form. The technoaesthetic prefers the surprising to the predictable: this is why it is diametrically opposed to technocracy.

The technoaesthetic resides half-way between the sacred and the technical. It is perfectly positioned to unite the two. On one side it is tied to the sacred: it has the sense of that which is given, of value and uniqueness. It aims for a beautiful totality. The world burgeons with its 'key points': promontories, mountains, the places where two rivers meet. On the other side, this aesthetic is operative. It creates, using craft, artifice and technologies. It gains mastery over matter and forms it into something new. In Simondon's eyes, this aesthetic is a bridge between these two conflicting experiences. It preserves the sense of the unique and the penchant for construction. For Simondon, aesthetics rank higher than ethics.

Plato reflected on questions of goodness and beauty in his *Hippias Major*. This dialogue teaches that the beautiful and the useful belong to two different orders. They may overlap, but it is a mistake to conflate the two. A ship is beautiful as it sails into a channel. Nevertheless, Plato's question concerns the vessel's storage rooms. Like a toga-clad customs agent who won't stand for any funny business, he demands to know what product is being transported in the ship's hold: is it good or bad for the city? Thus begin the endless discussions and inspections. The city cannot afford to place its confidence in an aesthetic sentiment. It may be no more than a mask. The same argument may be levelled at Simondon. He gives a poignant example of technoaesthetics: 'A dagger is only truly beautiful when it is in the hand that holds it'.[15] Is the beauty of the gesture sufficient to prevent a crime?

Aldous Huxley's *Brave New World* is a meditation on the beautiful and the good in a technocratic society. This brave new world has a singular beauty. Embryos are factory-made and population levels kept constant. Work is distributed according to the capabilities of the workers; pleasure is mass-produced. Everything is in its place. Every desire has an object. No friction disrupts the workings of the social machine. It maintains a controlled harmony. Ugliness is confined to the other side of the border, on Mexican reservations where idle natives read Shakespeare. Satirist and ironist, Huxley depicts a totalitarianism that is beautiful but cruel. Its harmony is troubled by a moral question. The aesthetic begins to crack. The savage demands freedom: freedom of books, freedom of invention, freedom of meaning. But everything functions perfectly without it, explains the Resident World Controller Mustapha Mond. He fears for the optimal beauty of his society. And so the savage becomes ugly but authentic: 'I'm claiming the right to be *unhappy*.' It is all that remains for him. One could not imagine a more human cry, nor one more at odds with technoaesthetics. But society has the means to grant this right: imprisonment.

All signs seem to indicate that the technoaesthetic is a philosophical wager, far from ready to be put into practice as the basis for any ethical or political system worthy of the name. It's the old story

---

[15] *Mode d'existence*, p. 186.

of how all things may be used for good or bad ends. It is impossible to conceive of a political system based on aesthetic impressions that emanate from the contemplation of a means to an end. Some may become aroused when presented with images of a technological scenography; others may attempt to make it serve a noble purpose. The technoaesthetic is nevertheless at the centre of Simondon's thought where it continues to beckon to us, even as it emerges in certain contemporary technologies.

12

Three Philosophers and *The Matrix*

Are we giving technologies too much credit? After all, they are only a means to an end. Do they really change our lives? Are modifications of material conditions really all that important, or are they merely phenomena, that is to say, appearances? Let us imagine that we have been transported to the Château de Ferney, home of Voltaire, in the middle of the eighteenth century. We are certain to feel out of our element. The food, transportation, correspondence and bathing arrangements would come as a shock. We could adapt, but it would be a different universe for us. Nevertheless, upon speaking with Voltaire we would find that the questions that preoccupy him are the same as ours. Life, death, fraternity, power, doubt, love, God. Little has changed. It is as if, through all of the radical modifications in conditions, the questions have continued to reverberate, unchanging, from one era to the next. The answers haven't fundamentally changed either. Increases in life expectancy have not robbed death of its mystery. We now have the vocabulary to formulate the question in purely physical terms. We may speak of senescence and cell death; the question loses neither its harshness nor its metaphysical prestige. Formulated in different terms it remains opaque. We could say the same of birth and of all the fundamental conditions of life. There is no surgical procedure by which to dissect the soul, though we may glimpse it in the eyes of the other. There is an irreducible store of questions and meanings that remain always intact. This is the well spring of true culture, which allows us, as we end a call on a cellular phone, to find our minds suddenly in empathy with the prehistoric frescos of the Lascaux caves. There is a thread that traverses history. Its permanence defies time. As we consider this enduring thread, progress may appear to be no more than a surface agitation.

Is there such a thing as moral progress? Pierre Larousse asked himself this very question in his *Universal Dictionary of the 19th Century* (*Dictionnaire universel du XIXe siècle*). He was moved to compose a panegyric. In almost every domain, he confirms, conditions have improved: materially, socially, in literature and art, in education. This is bound to continue, he writes, a man happy to live in his own time, a man whose imagination caresses a future which he will have helped to build. But at the end of the article a note of sober reflection creeps in to temper his enthusiasm. There are no more geniuses today than there were in previous times … It's a sort of fatalism. And then the moral: it must be acknowledged that there are as many morally 'obtuse' people today as there were yesterday. Likewise for the intellectually 'obtuse'. There is nothing to be done on this account, even if progress in education and material conditions *should* favour the moral improvement of society. Larousse thus has something like a nagging suspicion of a constant. He cannot manage to find a relationship of cause and effect between technical progress and moral progress. One rock resists erosion in the river of time. Always true to its own nature, it serves as a foundation for humanity.

Among the philosophers who have radicalized the suspicion articulated by Larousse, there is one who merits particular attention: Jankélévitch. For him, morality is the anti-technology, anti-capitalism and anti-matter *par excellence*. It operates according to a radically different logic. Technologies belong to the order of the available and the cumulative. We watch their growth as we would the returns on a profitable investment. Technology is something tangible, palpable. But morality … it is a sort of anti-matter, because the moment we

seize it – or think we have it in our hand – it is gone. Jankélévitch is
a theoretician of the fleeting and of the transient. He is in search of
a treasure that disappears the moment it is found, leaving a glimmer
that lodges in the heart. He is hunting for gold he doesn't expect to
find. More precisely, he is hunting for gold that is not material. It is
the gold of pure simplicity. His entire oeuvre is a quest for virtue,
accompanied by the paradoxical caveat that a virtue, once identified,
can never be possessed. Sincerity, for example, may be conquered
but never claimed. Whoever says 'I'm sincere' immediately ceases to
be, just as the pronouncement 'I've got a good sense of humour' will
inevitably elicit a certain scepticism. Jankélévitch's search for virtue
is not framed in terms of the usual bourgeois trade-off: there is none
of the self-satisfaction of those 'investors in virtue' who claim to have
found it. He speaks of Egyptian sarcophagi which sometimes bear
the inscription 'I am pure'.[1] Only the dead could claim to possess this
quality. The mortal who would venture to make this claim is surely
confusing the orders of capital with those of morality, the orders of
technology with those of virtue.

Jankélévitch uncompromisingly settles the question by separating
these orders. To confuse them would be perilous. *Being* and *having*
differ in every possible way. Being is emptied of all substance, while
having accumulates. More than a spirit of poverty, it is a nakedness.
The Greeks called the Indian Brahmins gymnosophists; that is,
etymologically, 'naked sages'. Theirs is the path of wisdom because
they are attached to nothing in particular, and yet they are connected
to everything, to life. The condition of love exists in detachment,
and in particular detachment from the self, in the struggle against
φιλαυτία (*philautia*), 'self-love'. The nakedness of the sage. But
technologies clothe us; each day they add new layers. Networks,
objects, prostheses, social security numbers, membership cards – the

---

[1] Cf. V. Jankélévitch, *Le pur et l'impur*, Paris: Flammarion, 1960.

body decks itself out with extensions too vast to be measured. Where does the human body end if we accept that the networks to which it is connected are its prosthetic extensions? Bergson, whose philosophy greatly influenced Jankélévitch, speaks of technologies as a physical swelling (*enflement physique*).[2] Progress, despite its etymological meaning, is not a step forward. It is an unfurling, a spreading outward. Mechanical muscles, electronic nerves, metallic hands, electric veins, plasma-screen eyes, amplified ears: each sense and each function finds a material amplification. Technology is the body, amplified. But what soul inhabits it? How could a tiny human soul, this *animula, vagula, blandula* that Marcus Aurelius spoke of, this tiny, white, vagabond soul, inhabit a body that has taken on almost planetary proportions? This is an enormous question. When Bergson calls for a 'supplement of soul (*supplément d'âme*)', he does not mean that technology destroys the soul. It would be a sign of neurosis to believe that by entering a car, the human being becomes an inanimate body surrounded by inert accessories. No, the soul persists, but as the body swells it reaches such incommensurate proportions that one might well worry about the distribution of the soul within that body. Bergson, in his work for the League of Nations, sensed that the early signs of globalization called for a new vitality: a morality and a religion which he described as dynamic, to indicate that their task was to move beyond the insularity of the clan mentality.

Jankélévitch, as we have noted, is Bergson's inheritor. He radicalizes Bergson's thought. Bergson calls for a supplement of soul, but never severs the ties between the technical order and the moral order, or between the mechanical order and the mystical order. Jankélévitch, for his part, adopts a more vigorous approach. Let the body swell. But, in that case, don't expect it to be virtuous. There is no virtue in

---

[2] Cf. H. Bergson, *Les deux sources de la morale et de la religion. Remarques finales sur la mécanique et la mystique*, Paris: P.U.F., 1973 (1st edn 1932).

an inflated or artificially enhanced musculature. He had his reasons, not least among them the concentration camps and the technologies on which they relied. Jankélévitch's path leads towards music, joy and simplicity. He borrows Bergson's word *intuition* to indicate that these ecstasies reconnect us with the heart of life. It is interesting to note that Simondon is also an attentive reader of Bergson. He knows him perfectly. His entire oeuvre may be seen as a game of light and sound that mirrors and echos the author of *Creative Evolution* (*l'Évolution créatrice*). Themes of becoming, the individual, evolution, matter and memory are common to both authors. But if Jankélévitch radicalizes Bergson's thought, Simondon revolutionizes it.

Simondon takes Bergson to task for his '*aristocratism*'.[3] He asks: Why these privileges? Why keep matter and technology in a situation of inferiority while elevating the spirit to such lofty heights? Does nothing happen, then, within the realm of matter? And what are technologies if not the product of human labours, efforts and ingenuity that overcome the limits of the physical? Why these two classes? Bergson had anticipated this objection. *Creative Evolution* is organized as a defence against these criticisms. There is a strict hierarchy, explains Bergson, because intelligence and intuition have different functions and qualities. Intelligence, that faculty of the *Homo sapiens* that developed as human beings refined their tools, is oriented towards the material world. It arranges, organizes and segments matter. It constructs huts or buildings; regardless of the level of complexity, at its origin the procedure is always the same: look at the material, invent a form, impose the form on matter. Technology is a game played with modelling clay or Lego bricks. However grandiose it may be its limits are the same, because it does not engage with the noblest manifestations of the human spirit. Besides, technology is locked in struggle. It is reactive. It tries to turn the situation to its own

---

[3] *L'individu et sa genèse*, p. 267.

advantage because, fundamentally, it is animated by the impression that nature is against it. It may well be right! Nakedness in the desert … Jules Verne again comes to mind: in *Michael Strogoff: The Courier of the Czar* (original French title: *Michel Strogoff*), Strogoff's journey to Irkutsk surrounded by hostile elements – fire, ice and bears – requires strategic gambits. But the fact remains that technology braces itself against life. Shoulder to shoulder, intelligence and life each defend their interests, which do not converge. Intuition, in contrast, is like a blind leap, or a grace. It ceases to fight; it lets itself be taken. Stop thinking, stop wanting to organize and control. Let yourself go. Feel the vital impetus (élan vital), a certain harmony between the universe and a *self* which has ceased to view itself as a solitary atom lost in the immensity of the world. In Bergson's conception of intuition there is a quest for symbiosis, a reunion with a primitive simplicity which represents the pinnacle of evolution. Intelligence is a purgatory and a necessity. Beyond it, and on a completely separate plane, human intuition rediscovers an effortless peace. It does not fight against the current. It has found the right position. The intuitive human is all the more joyful, since whatever she gives to life, life returns to her a hundredfold: dreams, music, love.

Simondon, fascinated by this promise, enthralled by this facility, and, undoubtedly, having experienced it for himself, adds his two cents. Or rather, he asks: Why not me, why not them? Why wouldn't these technological outcasts also have the right to some small portion of this ecstasy? Simondon demands it. First of all, Bergson is a believer in universal brotherhood. His morality and his religion promise that no one will be left by the wayside. And certainly not by some a priori decision which presents itself as incontestable. The edict is unjust; this ostracism is abusive. Why should those who build, who maintain, who explore the universe and return with images of stars and oceans, why should they be denied the right to participate in this intuition? Is the explorer who decides to take up residence in the Chilean mountains in order to observe the passage of comets merely intelligent? Is he only an orchestrator? Nonetheless, he has cosmic intuitions. Furthermore, says Simondon, we must not get our terms confused. Yes, technocracy exists, capitalism is destructive, and often objects, in the way that they are sold or produced, create barriers between social groups. A certain type of technology closes off society, pushing it towards the unpromising path of desire and luxury. Objects serve to mark boundary lines and often become a fortifying wall for egoism and a stronghold for vacuous contentment based on mindless consumption. But Simondon asks that these behaviours, which result from the malignity of manipulators of opinion and the fragility of judgement, not be conflated with a different type of technology, for which he demands greater consideration. This plea on behalf of technology is the millstone around his neck. It is perhaps because of this that he was, in his own time, so often misunderstood or dismissed out of hand, especially since the Marxist intelligentsia of the time saw the spectre of Roosevelt or Nixon behind the word 'technology'. Yet, as we have already pointed out, Simondon was as much a critic of capitalism as he was of Marxism. At a time when cold war mentalities dominated, he offered, in their stead, the intuition of a man attentive to the consequences of his actions. He wrote to the President of the United States to demand the release of the Rosenbergs. In India he studied networks of food distribution. He requested, therefore, that he be given the benefit of the doubt regarding this exception, and that it be examined closely: to confirm whether the problems posed by technologies might at root be problems of mentality, of pollution in pursuit of profit, of idle curiosities, etc.

To demand that Bergsonian intuition be applied to the relation with matter and technologies is no insignificant act. Jankélévitch would have been furious. But this is what Simondon does. In his pages on crystallography he shows that the crystal is an individual, which Bergson explicitly denies.[4] More profoundly, this means that the physico-chemical processes of matter cannot be reduced to simple 'arrangements'. For Simondon, matter is possessed of life. In the same way he speaks of technical 'individuals': intelligence is not sufficient to comprehend a process of creative invention. This revolution is undoubtedly a usurpation. It battles against the most ancient and entrenched of hierarchies. Common sense would never validate it. Deaf to the pronouncements of common sense, and often forgetful of the fact that philosophy is far too important an affair to be left in the hands of philosophers – or scientists! – Simondon pushes radically against the current. In this regard he seems to have been intent on marginality. His demand is exorbitant, but it may possibly have a positive effect.

The Matrix, among other examples of science fiction films, gives us an opportunity to pose the question of intelligence and intuition in the technological world. At the beginning of the twenty-first century the world is at peace, and human beings have developed a new generation of intelligent machines. At the same time, and without any clear indication as to whether humans or machines are the cause, the sky darkens – everywhere, clouds and rain. Machines, previously fuelled by solar energy, must find an alternate energy source or perish. But this already implies that these *artificial intelligences* are not merely intelligent. They have the *intuition* that their mode of existence is threatened, and to protect themselves they subjugate a humanity that has grown too confident and has delegated too many of its own capacities to these machines. Human bodies, from this point on, vegetate in vats of reddish water while their corporeal energy serves to fuel a cybernetic population that continues to develop as before. The relations of service are inverted; humankind has become

---

[4] Cf. H. Bergson, *Évolution créatrice*, Paris: P.U.F. (1st edn 1941), 1989, p. 12; published in English as *Creative Evolution*, trans. Arthur Mitchell.

a source of energy, on which the machines are so dependent that they flatter and maintain it by giving humans the illusion that they continue to live, laugh and labour, even as their bodies float immobile in a vat of liquid. *The Matrix* is the computer-generated illusion, the programme that reformats the human brain and generates a collective hallucination. Corporeal hell, artificial paradise for human beings: their atrophied bodies lead a lethargic existence while their minds submit to the virtual simulation of a mediocre but peaceful existence. *1984, Brave New World, The Matrix* and many other apocalyptic, futuristic projections indicate that the price of technological progress is mass delusion. Our minds inhabit a magical theatre that lacks a physical reality: *esse est percipi*; the matrix is an extension of Berkeley's philosophy. But humanity is cheated of all of the fundamental life experiences: birth, friendship, love, death. Such is the illusive power of technology. It is a strange reversal: the more we delegate intelligence to technology in artificial form, the more our intuition is diminished. The fundamentals are obscured from view.

So, are Simondon's requests and the path he follows irresponsible? If the greatest geniuses of science fiction deploy their talents to play the role of Cassandra, if common sense itself attempts to alter its course and shows evidence of a fear that is genuine but impossible to name, these are signs of a great mistrust and uneasiness. This philosophy is faced with fear. What memory, then, should we retain of Simondon concerning these questions to which he gives no answer, since the only answers are part of an attitude? That of an honest man in an age of technology, a man who opposes oppression, a man literally *seized* by an awareness of the human facility for creating slaves and exploiting the gestures of others. That of an optimist who calls for a reform of the conception of labour, because our societies have lost in passion what they have gained in mechanism. And what about joy, we might ask. A strange question! A weighty demand! Isn't the real problem the fact that we are asking this of technology? That we forget to look for it in human beings?

Index